God's Goodness &
Our Mindfulness

RESPONDING VERSUS REACTING TO

Life Changing Circumstances

Ervin (Earl) Cobb
Charlotte D. Grant-Cobb, PhD

ALSO BY

Ervin (Earl) Cobb
and
Charlotte D. Grant-Cobb, PhD

BOOKS

Living a Richer Life:
Getting the Most out of Life's Gifts and Circumstances

Focused Leadership:
What You Can Do Today to Become a More Effective Leader

Pillow Talk Consciousness:
Intimate Reflections on America's 100 Most Interesting
Thoughts and Suspicions

Navigating the Life Enrichment Model™

Until I Change

VIDEO PROGRAMS

Get Ready to Reap All the Richness Your Life Has to Offer

All of the above are available at your local bookstore or may be ordered by visiting:
www.richerlifeassociates.com

God's Goodness & Our Mindfulness

RESPONDING VERSUS REACTING TO

Life Changing Circumstances

✠RICHER Press
An Imprint of Richer Life, LLC

Copyright © 2012 by Richer Life, LLC

Published by ╫RICHER Press
An Imprint of Richer Life, LLC

4600 E. Washington Street, Suite 300, Phoenix, Arizona 85034
www.richerlifeassociates.com

Cover Design: Richer Media USA

RICHER Press books and products are available through most bookstores. RICHER Press also publishes its books in a variety of electronic formats. Some content that appears in print may not be available in electronic books.

Library of Congress Cataloging-in-Publications Data

God's Goodness & Our Mindfulness:
Responding Versus Reacting to
Life Changing Circumstances
Ervin (Earl) Cobb and Charlotte D. Grant-Cobb -- 1st edition
p.   cm.

1. Self-Help   2. Christian Education   3. Life Enrichment
ISBN 978-0-9744617-8-6 (pbk : alk. Paper)

2012903264

ISBN 13: 978-0-9744617-8-6
ISBN 10: 0-9744617-8-6

Text set is Adobe Garamond

PRINTED IN THE UNITED STATES OF AMERICA

First edition
April 2012

ACKNOWLEDGEMENTS

We would like to extend special thanks to all of those who have used the *Life Enrichment Model*™ to make better choices and shape positive outcomes to life changing circumstances and were kind enough to share their experiences with us.

CONTENTS

PREFACE

Could you have avoided costly mistakes in your life if you knew then what you know now? If you could make the outcome of one of your most crucial life decisions more positive, would you do it? A great number of people would seize the opportunity to make a good decision even better.

That's one of the reasons many gravitated to *Living a Richer Life: Getting the Most out of Life's Gifts and Circumstances*. In their first book, Earl Cobb and his wife, Dr. Charlotte Grant-Cobb, constructed the *Life Enrichment Model* [TM] to provide you with a tool to enhance your ability to more consciously respond to major circumstances in your life. In developing the model, however, Charlotte and Earl noted that even the best tools can't give you peace in the midst of a crisis.

So in their sequel, *God's Goodness and Our Mindfulness*, the Cobbs, for the first time, share the source of their belief that *"responding versus reacting to life's most challenging circumstances results in more positive outcomes."* In their usual, instructive and descriptive manner, Earl and Charlotte illustrate, through the use of two of the most preeminent stories in the Bible, the importance of recognizing God's goodness and responding mindfully when confronting life altering circumstances.

By reading this book you will be encouraged by knowing that (a) God's Goodness always reveals the magnitude of the circumstance and (b) responding mindfully to all circumstances in your life invites God's presence and grace.

Furthermore, you will be fortified by the presentation of uplifting narratives that demonstrate the application of faith and mindfulness to crucial life altering circumstances.

Additionally, you will be presented with the opportunity to learn more about the *consciousness-enhancing* nature of the Life Enrichment Model ™ and how to properly apply the model to a potentially life changing circumstance in your life.

INTRODUCTION

As many of our readers are aware, we do not consider ourselves self-improvement gurus or psychological geniuses. We are just two hard working Americans who grew up in working class families. We, like millions of working class Americans, were fortunate enough to raise a healthy family, work our way through college and work hard enough to carve out rewarding careers. We were also fortunate enough to build a network of friends and business acquaintances that have been instrumental in providing emotional and spiritual support.

However, we both have had a life-long interest in improving ourselves, our lives and the lives of those around us. Over the years, we have not viewed our personal or professional improvement projects as laborious tasks but as practical ways to use our own minds to broaden our perspective of life and the world we share with billions of others.

It has been over ten years since we first started our largest and most comprehensive project. This particular project led us to the creation of a chronicle which frames and highlights the major events that have occurred throughout much of our lifetime. To our surprise, we were able to document the events in somewhat excruciating detail. The events cover nearly thirty years of life and marriage.

This revealing chronicle allowed us to deeply reflect on how we were able to influence the outcomes of many of the *life changing circumstances* which surrounded those events. The chronicle and our work laid the foundation for the development of the Life Enrichment Model™ and the first book we wrote

11

together, *Living a Richer Life: Getting the Most out of Life's Gifts and Circumstances.*

It has also been over a year since we published *Living a Richer Life.* Following numerous book reviews, book signings and personal appearances across the United States, we have had a chance to reflect on the book itself and the impact it is having on a cadre of individuals and families.

From the feedback we have received, the one thing that really stands out is the significant value that the Life Enrichment Model™ has provided to men and women of all persuasions. Based on the comments and testimonials we have received, it is apparent that many of those needing to respond more effectively to potentially life changing circumstances have embraced the Life Enrichment Model™. An overwhelming number of them have found it to be a friendly and effective tool.

The one question that we have been asked most often during discussions regarding our first book is — *"What do you believe were the primary forces driving the outcomes you experienced in the personal narratives included in your book?*

You would think that after spending years compiling our chronicle and several more years constructing the manuscript which resulted in the writing of *Living a Richer Life,* we would have had an immediate response to this question. To the contrary, for almost a year, we could not provide a concise response.

A few months ago, while spending a few days together in the chilly mountains of Northern Arizona, we found some time to expand the search of our inner thoughts and explore a proper response to this question. After a few hours of reflecting on our life chronicle, the personal narratives included in *Living a Richer Life* and many of the insights we shared in the book, we both arrived at the same response…and here it is.

We believe that the primary forces that drove many of the outcomes to the personal circumstances we detailed in *Living a Richer Life* can be best described as *God's Goodness* and *Our Mindfulness.*

In light of the dozens of concepts discussed in *Living a Richer Life* — ranging from the Life Enrichment Continuum™ and the power of self-awareness to the natural patterns of human behavior — you might ask how we arrived at *God's Goodness* and *Our Mindfulness* as the primary forces that have driven and continue to drive our responses to life altering circumstances.

Well, in this book we answer that question. We also present what we believe is our most straight forward and, hopefully, convincing case as to why responding versus *reacting* to life changing circumstances will increase the probability of more positive outcomes in your life. We have included in *"God's Goodness and Our Mindfulness: Responding versus Reacting to Life Changing Circumstances"*, the same four personal narratives presented in *Living a Richer Life*. As a primer, we have also included an abridged version of the Life Enrichment Model™ Application Guide.

The personal narratives are taken directly from our life chronicle. They have been formatted to correspond with the *five stages* associated with the Life Enrichment Model™. In addition to being fortified and encouraged by the candid and detailed stories, you should view them as *examples* of the degree of detail you are seeking as the output (and insight) from each of the stages as you apply the Life Enrichment Model™ to a major circumstance in your life.

It is our hope that you will —like many others — become convinced that thoughtfully *responding* versus simply *reacting* to potentially life changing circumstances will generate more positive outcomes in your life.

It is our belief that you find the Life Enrichment Model™ to be a friendly and effective tool to assist you in getting into a position to mentally, psychologically and spiritually *respond* to all major circumstances in the future.

God's Goodness

Life changing circumstances arrive in our lives with varying degrees of severity. The use of a guide or model such as the Life Enrichment Model™ enhances our ability to deal with the difficulties and challenges they bring. However, the severity of the challenges in some circumstances will drop most of us to our knees. At those times, it is important to know that there is also a model that can enhance our capacity for *endurance* and *perseverance*. That model is God's Goodness.

Here is one biblical example which illustrates how understanding God's Goodness is a genuine guide to mindfully responding to difficult circumstances. It is a guide that we all inherit as children of God.

The story of Moses appears in the Bible, Torah, Talmud, Midrash and Quran. Apparently this story, that highlights man's ability to triumph over circumstances, resonates across faiths. Indeed, universal themes about life's circumstances can be found throughout the story of Moses:

- Moses provides examples of reacting versus responding to circumstances;
- Moses shows us that it is reasonable to expect God's Goodness;
- Moses shows us that God's Goodness is manifested in His Glory and
- Moses shows us that God's Goodness is equal to or greater than the demands of our circumstances.

How heartening it is to understand that God's Goodness is inseparable from His glory. Recall that Moses asked to see God's glory. "Then Moses said, I pray Thee, show me Thy

15

glory"! And He said, "I Myself will make all My goodness pass before you, and will proclaim the name of the LORD before you; and I will be gracious to whom I will be gracious, and will show compassion on whom I will show compassion" (Exodus 33:19).

By the time Moses asked to see God's glory, he had a clear sense of the magnitude of his circumstances. The conditions God revealed to Moses were nothing short of mind blowing. We can imagine that Moses reacted with a combination of awe and fear. Exodus 12:37 tells us, "And the people of Israel journeyed from Rameses to Succoth, about six hundred thousand men on foot, besides women and children." Scholars estimate that there were at least 2 million men, women and children at any given time during the exodus from Egypt. That's a circumstance that would engender a reaction of escaping from Egypt, alone, in the dead of night. Instead, Moses responded by praying and asking to see God's glory.

Many read this passage of the Bible and think that Moses must have been pretty confident of his relationship with God to ask to see His glory, but the opposite was true. In fact, Moses was so sure that knowing more of God was a prerequisite for undertaking the journey that he said to the Lord, "If you don't personally go with us, don't make us leave this place" (Exodus 33:15).

In other words, Moses knew that the only reasoned response to a circumstance as great as the exodus was God's Goodness and glory. Moses, remember, died at 120 years of age. So he was in his late eighties or early 90s when he and the Israelites started on their journey. Prior to that he was in the desert 40 years and prior to that he was a prince in Egypt. In other words, Moses did not grow up always studying the God of the Israelites. He did not have the luxury of a lengthy evidence-based faith walk, like Abraham. There was a big gap in his knowledge of the One upon whom he would be most dependent.

16

Certainly, Moses believed he was called by God to the work. But he was also clear that the very real need to feed, clothe and protect several million people required real and reasoned responses. Moses, at the age of 40, acted on instinct, without regard for the consequences, and killed the Egyptian. The consequences of not evaluating that situation were a death on his conscious and 40 years in the desert. So even though it was God who revealed the circumstances of the exodus to Moses, he needed to assess the situation and make an informed decision about how best to proceed. Moses understood that as daunting as the revelations of his circumstances were, he could not trust the outcomes to his reactions. He concluded that only by knowing more of God would he have the ability and confidence to trust in Him.

Apparently God thought that it was reasonable for Moses to desire to know more of Him. God actually wanted Moses to have the assurance that he would supply a magnitude of His goodness and glory that was equal to or greater than the demand of the circumstances. We find example upon example of God's Goodness manifesting throughout the wilderness journey. For the entire forty years we are told that they were provided with food in the form of manna.

On two occasions, when the people complained they had no meat, God met that demand with quail. Their clothes and shoes never wore out. Moses asked to see God's glory and he saw it by day and by night. "By day the Lord went ahead of them in a pillar of cloud to guide them on their way and by night in a pillar of fire to give them light, so that they could travel by day or night. Neither the pillar of cloud by day nor the pillar of fire by night left its place in front of the people" (Exodus 13:21-22).

From the story of Moses, we have come to understand that when God reveals circumstances, even unbelievable circumstances, he also hears our prayers and supplications.

17

Through Moses he affirmed for us that it is reasonable to expect Him to supply us with His goodness and glory equal to or greater than the demand of our circumstances. More importantly, this story affirms for us that God's presence and goodness, manifested through his glory, will stay with us through the entire season of any circumstance.

Our Mindfulness

Our mindfulness or awareness of God's Goodness anchors both the responses and the outcomes to difficult circumstances. Being mindful of the manifestations of God's Goodness restores confidence in our responses and our ability to execute the plan required to positively shape outcomes to many of life's circumstances. This confidence is a powerful conduit for giving and receiving guidance and support.

In this regard, we are reminded of the biblical story of Mary. Her story appears as a model of mindfulness which linked God's Goodness to her daily activities and interactions.

When Mary, the mother of Christ Jesus, thought of how God had been mindful of her, she glorified and rejoiced about the goodness of God. "And Mary said: My soul glorifies the Lord and my spirit rejoices in God my Savior, for he has been mindful of the humble state of his servant" (Luke 1:46-55).

Those who know the Bible are not surprised to read David's song, in Psalms 8:4, "What is man that you are mindful of him, and the son of man, that you care for him." After all, David was created to compose and sing at the presence of even one little drop of God's Goodness and mercy. It is much more difficult to find passages that depict Mary as a singer/psalmist. But Mary was compelled to "break forth in song" because she was able to make the link between God's mindfulness, his blessings and his goodness toward her.

Her communication with her older relative Elizabeth has been proclaimed, *The Magnificat,* and is referred to as *Mary's Song.* Mary's response to God's mindfulness helps us understand that the practice of mindfulness is an appropriate response to

God's Goodness. Her response suggests that only when our mindfulness results in rejoicing, is there a link with God's Goodness. In fact, the development of a practice of mindfulness that emulates God's mindfulness strengthens our ability to thoughtfully *respond* rather than merely *react* to life changing circumstances. The practice of mindfulness significantly enhances the probability of positive outcomes because:

- Our mindfulness of God's Goodness enables his presence to infiltrate and illuminate every circumstance; and

- Our mindfulness of God's Goodness provides so much joy that others involved in the circumstance are also blessed by association.

We define the practice of mindfulness as the practice of witnessing your circumstances without inserting your emotions, perspectives or experiences into the content prior to clearly understanding the surrounding realities. Across the planet, various faiths are hard at work teaching the practice of mindfulness to earnest learners. We found the best way to develop a mindfulness practice that emulates God's mindfulness is to follow the biblical models. It is the model that Mary used. It is the model her son used. It is initiated by actively worshiping God and it is enriched by loving others.

Mary had a practice of being obedient to God. Luke tells us that she was not alarmed to see an angel of God in her home. Mary had to be engaged in an active practice of obedience, because we are told God found favor with her. It is unlikely that she would have called her obedience mindfulness, but indeed it was. Even though Mary's life was about to change dramatically, God was with her. Just as God revealed the magnitude of the approaching situation to Moses, He revealed the same to Mary. The angel said, "The Lord is with you." Whenever the words, "The Lord is with you" appear in scripture, an invitation from God to be part of His plan is attached. Recall in Exodus 3:12, God tells Moses, "I will be with you." Similarly, in Jeremiah 1:8,

20

we see God invite Jeremiah to his challenge, "Do not be afraid of them, for I am with you and will rescue you, declares the Lord."

It is our desire for the presence of the Lord to infiltrate and illuminate each and every circumstance we encounter along the *Continuum of Life*. Therefore our mindfulness incorporates a continuous practice of worshipping the Lord. We want God to find favor with us, so we worship Him with our whole heart and soul as we are commanded to do in Deuteronomy 6:5. Our mindfulness practice also helps us facilitate positive outcomes by sharing God's Goodness with others. By thinking of other's needs, we have found a key to linking God's Goodness to our mindfulness.

As you read the personal narratives from our life chronicle, we hope you see our mindfulness in practice. As you apply the Life Enrichment Model™ to a circumstance in your life, remember that God's Goodness and your mindfulness will *enhance* your ability to get the most from the tool — and fortify your efforts to shape more positive outcomes.

This enhancement is critical to the process of effectively responding to major circumstances because even the best tools can't give you peace in the midst of a crisis.

"Mindfulness lets us absorb the richness of the moment. We believe that the self-awareness that comes through mindfulness drives us to be more intentional in choosing the priorities and actions that best fit our life's mission."

Ervin (Earl) Cobb and
Charlotte D. Grant-Cobb, PhD

Life Changing Circumstances

Getting a good grasp of the role that *events* and *circumstances* play in your life is essential to you understanding how to shape more positive outcomes to challenging situations. Achieving this level of consciousness is also essential to you recognizing and valuing the difference between *responding* versus simply *reacting* to a circumstance.

For various reasons, many of us have not thought a lot about the difference between a life event and a life circumstance. Prior to writing our first book, *Living a Richer Life* we had not given it much thought either.

However, through our research for the book and close reflection upon a number of major events and circumstances from our past — we discovered that for many years we had actually used an inherent process that recognized and valued such a distinction. It became apparent that by doing so, we benefitted greatly from how we internalized the events and how we responded to the surrounding circumstances.

Let's start by answering the question, "What distinguishes a life event from a life circumstance?" Then, we will discuss why recognizing and valuing this distinction can make a significant difference in how you view the circumstance and your ability to shape a more positive outcome.

Most events in life are fairly common. Most result in minor changes in your life and in your lifestyle. However, there are events that can cause significant turmoil and change in your life. Among them, we would include:

- A marriage;
- The birth of a child;

23

- A major salary increase;
- Becoming the caretaker of an aging parent;
- The purchase of a new home;
- A felony DWI conviction;
- The death of a spouse;
- A long-term loss of employment;
- A permanent disability;
- A chronic illness;
- An early retirement;
- A home foreclosure;
- Personal bankruptcy;
- A teenage pregnancy; and
- Winning of the lottery.

Some of these events are planned. Some even fall into the category of life accomplishments. Others, unfortunately, are the result of being in the wrong place at the wrong time. While others appear to be curve balls thrown at you and can suddenly seem unfair, unclear and certainly unexpected.

Now, circumstances, on the other hand, are conditions or facts that determine [or must be considered in determining] a course of action. Circumstances, in most cases, are the result of a single event or a sequence of events that can change our daily existence. What was once so easily in our grasp, such as a promising career, a beautiful home or a loving friend, can disappear in an instant. However, it is also true that circumstances can serve as powerful catalysts. They can assist you in enacting and realizing significant changes in your life.

Many people unconsciously forfeit their ability to understand and control the outcomes caused by major events that unexpectedly surface in their lives. They do this, all too often, by reacting versus responding to the circumstances surrounding the event. Some of them act as if it's an inevitable conclusion that they will suffer a periled consequence, lose something that is special to them or feel a certain way based on a particular set of circumstances.

However, did you know that in almost every case it is not the actual event itself that causes life's most challenging ups and downs? The cause of the most helpful and the most harmful life changes you experience as a consequence of a major life event is how you internalize what the event means to you and your response to the circumstances that accompany the event.

For example, a teenage pregnancy is accompanied by circumstances which could involve addressing the need to complete a good education and to find the wherewithal not to allow an early life event to derail career and lifelong aspirations. The winning of a cash lottery can become *unrewarding* unless timely investment, relationship and privacy management steps are taken to address circumstances which may cause a *bigger purse* to turn into an even *bigger headache*. With your proactive and well-planned response, the outcome to each of these events [an unexpected pregnancy and winning the lottery] could enrich your life and the lives of people around you. Without such a response, dreams could be lost and relationships could be ruined for a lifetime.

When you more thoughtfully respond versus simply react to circumstances which surface as a result of an event, you can more effectively shape a desired outcome. You can also minimize negative impacts that life's inevitable events may have on the quality of your life and the lives of people you love.

Armed with a clear understanding of the significance of the event, a well-crafted response and the control of your humanistic gifts, you can seize potential opportunities which are embedded within life's inevitable circumstances.

Even though the concept of *reacting* versus *responding* to major circumstances may appear naturally obvious, it is not as easy as it seems. Most people instinctively "react" to surprises and unexpected changes in their life.

As we all get older, we become conditioned by customs and our daily environment. This conditioning, in many cases, allows pre-determined reactions to replace more mindful responses. In addition, many of us tend to not recognize the institutional influences which are at odds with our ability to gain broader perspectives of important situations and respond in a manner which shapes the most positive outcomes.

In the last section of this book, you will find a discussion of a paradigm we constructed to assist you in your understanding of the various environmental and human behavioral factors that come into play when you encounter major circumstances in your life. The paradigm is called the *Life Enrichment Continuum*™. We suggest that you spend some time reviewing the "Enrichment Principles" and "Enrichment Challenges" set forth in the Life Enrichment Continuum™. Integrating concepts similar to those presented in this paradigm into your thought process can help you recognize influences which may be preventing you from more effectively responding to major circumstances in your life.

By doing so, you will significantly increase the number of positive outcomes in your life, minimize the number of negative outcomes and live a richer and more abundant life.

The Journey and the Discovery

As we mentioned in the Introduction, it has been over a decade since we initiated one of our most thought-provoking and revealing projects. The project turned out to be quite a journey. It unknowingly led us to greatly appreciate an insightful observation --- when we are in the *position* to thoughtfully respond versus just react to life altering circumstances, we tend to make better choices and shape more positive outcomes.

In this section, we share with you an overview of our extremely revealing journey. We also provide a brief description and the basic premise surrounding the process or model we discovered along the way which is designed to help you get into the position to make better life choices and shape more positive outcomes.

The Journey

The original goal of this project was to enlighten ourselves on how well we navigated through many of the challenges we had faced together during almost thirty years of married life. The project involved developing a chronicle to determine:

- How we responded to the circumstances we faced?

- How we arrived at the decisions we made? and

- What were the pluses and minuses associated with the actual outcomes?

When we started this journey we were [and still are] quite secure in our spiritual beliefs and the grace of God. Thus, we were not looking for answers as to "why" events in our lives had unfolded as they had --- good or bad. Through our Christian experience, we both have always known the *"goodness of God"* and who is in ultimate control. Our goal was to enlighten ourselves by examining the earthly factors involved in how we navigated through many of our life's challenges and opportunities.

We were acutely aware from our own life experiences that "societal dimensions or factors" [i.e. family-birth privileges, educational level, decision-making skills and relationships] along with how we innately respond to them, must have played a significant role in determining the outcomes we had experienced. The only questions in our minds were:

- *Which factors had the most influence and when?*

- *How much control, on a daily basis, do we have on affecting our behavior and life's outcomes?*

- *What governed our responses to our greatest challenges and circumstances? and*

- *Whether or not the "lessons we would learn" could be effectively shared with others?*

At the completion of the project, we were truly enlightened by how we responded to a number of the circumstances we faced over this period. In hindsight, there were many opportunities we might have missed as we raised our family, navigated through careers, addressed the needs of elderly parents and struggled with corporate downsizings.

As fate would have it, we thoroughly enjoyed the journey and were quite pleased and somewhat surprised by what it revealed. In satisfying our curiosity regarding the influence of societal factors on life's outcomes, we gained fresh insight about ourselves, our relationships and how our priorities in life had indeed influenced many significant outcomes. Moreover, our research and analysis revealed a unique view of a repeatable "pattern of events" and contemporary process associated with directly shaping more positive outcomes.

The Discovery

It was the discovery of this contemporary process or *model* which initially ignited our excitement around the writing our first book together, *Living a Richer: Getting the Most out of Life's Gifts and Circumstances.* The model is now known as the *Life Enrichment Model*™. A graphical depiction of the model is shown below.

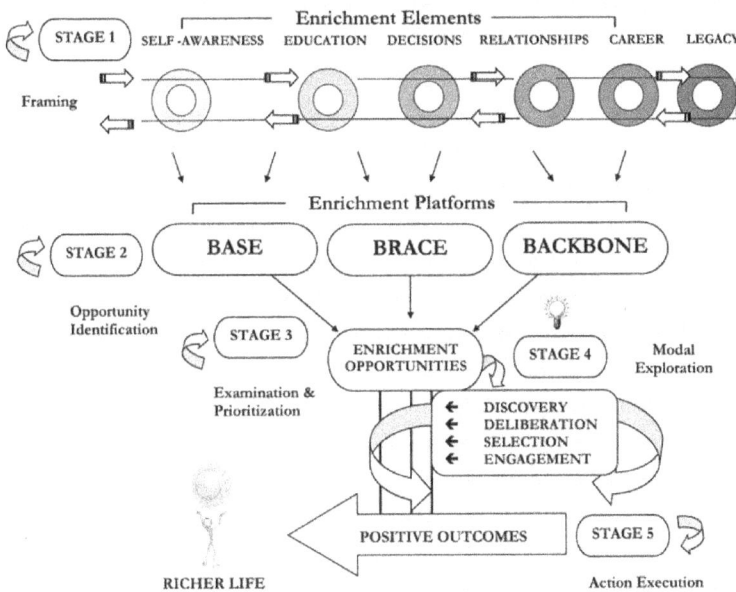

Graphical Depiction of the *Life Enrichment Model*™

When properly applied, the Life Enrichment Model™ can become an exceptional tool to aid in identifying unforeseen opportunities and determining the paths available to you as you encounter potentially life altering circumstances. The results of the model's queries can help you get into the *position* [mentally, psychologically and spiritually] to make better decisions, take appropriate actions and to more consciously make the adjustments required to formulate your responses to shape more positive outcomes.

The model's construct utilizes figurative depictions and characterizations to provide valuable insights into the intangibles in your life at the time you encounter a major circumstance. The depictions and characterizations are generalizations and should be used as a guide to *steer* you in a most probable direction. However, when you merge these *generalities* with your own timely observations and sound reasoning, the combination gives you a significant advantage as compared to simple *reacting* and *going it alone.*

The model combines an elevated level of consciousness, self-examination and critical thinking techniques to yield valuable insights for making good choices. Through repetitive and random evaluations, it is apparent that the model, when properly applied, is uniquely capable of consistently helping to ensure that we all can place ourselves in a *better position* to more effectively respond to potentially life changing circumstances.

In the *Life Enrichment Model*™" *Application Guide* located in the final section of this book, you will find a detailed discussion of the Life Enrichment Model™. We have included the guide to help you better understand the model's components and assist you in applying the model to circumstances that you may be encountering now or in the future.

Above all, allow yourself to be open to a new approach to thinking through challenging situations…and enjoy the journey.

Opportunities Revealed
Personal Narratives

The following narratives are formatted to correspond with the *five stages* associated with the Life Enrichment Model. In addition to being fortified and encouraged by the candid and detailed stories, you should view them as examples of the degree of detail you are seeking as the output (and insight) from each of the stages as you apply the Life Enrichment Model™ to a major circumstance in your life.

A NEW HOUSE FOR MOM AND DAD

MODAL EXPLORATION

Discovery

In the late 1980's, Earl's parents were in their late sixties. Starting in the mid-1970's they had developed a ritual of traveling to visit their children's homes. They would regularly travel between Arizona, Colorado, Nebraska, West Virginia, South Carolina and Florida for lengthy stays during hot summers and cold winters.

Earl's parents visiting
Phoenix in 1989

However, by 1989, there were few trips being made. They also appeared to be slowing down. They shared with us that they were not up to fighting the crowds at the airports anymore and wanted to sleep in their own bed.

After Mom barely survived a serious case of pneumonia during the winter of 1991, Earl and I both became extremely concerned about their health. We were as concerned about their ability to properly maintain their health in the Cobb family's house located in the small Mid-Georgia town of Vienna. Vienna is located about 140 miles due south of Atlanta, just off of Interstate I-75. Similar to most small towns in the South, it did

33

not have many local services and reached its maximum population of around 4,000 back in the late 1950's.

Artice and Carrie Bell Cobb with Earl's youngest sister, Selma, in front of Cobb family home in 1955

The Cobb family's home was built by Earl's dad during the evenings and on the weekends in the early 1950's. It was a small, four room house. This is where Earl was born and where his parents, Artice and Carrie Bell Cobb raised eight children.

Earl's father worked as a local painter, barber and handyman. He was also born in the Vienna area and only had the opportunity to obtain a fourth grade education. Earl's mom, affectionately called Carrie Bell, had a seventh grade education and was a stay-at-home mother. The only exception was that in order to make ends meet, she would occasionally take on an odd job cleaning other's homes and regularly performed seasonal work in the cotton fields during the summers. There never was much money. But, the home was always filled with love and wonderful memories. However, the house itself did not have central air or heat and was not suitable, in our minds, for our aging parents. The old home was also void of the space and amenities that we envisioned would be required as Earl and his seven siblings (and their children) would now need to regularly travel to Georgia to spend time with their aging parents in the coming years.

During this time, Earl was a group vice president with Motorola's Government and Systems Technology Group in Scottsdale, Arizona. He had just been promoted to head Motorola's world-wide military radio systems business unit. I was a vice president and senior manager with Norwest Bank in Phoenix. I was managing a large financial trust portfolio for the bank. Our only child, Brandi Reneè, was a teenager at the time. In other words, our personal financial situation was in fairly good shape. With our financial ability to address our parent's housing dilemma not being in question, we concluded the following:

Our Circumstance: If we do not improve the housing situation, it is possible that Mom would not survive another bout with pneumonia. The summer temperatures are presenting an increasing health threat to both Mom and Dad without adequate air conditioning. As they continue to age, they will not be able to safely light the old gas stove in the living room used to heat the entire house in the winter months. Furthermore, it is not certain that we will continue to have the financial fortunes and wherewithal to seriously address the dilemma that the lack of adequate housing would continue to present.

Our Opportunity: If it is our desire to improve Mom and Dad's housing situation, then now is the time to adequately respond to this circumstance. We could wait and react to the next bout of pneumonia or the next health issue. But, we both know that ignoring the root cause of the problem and simply reacting to the symptoms would not address our real concerns. By responding now, in a proactive and thoughtful manner, we would take advantage of our ability to finance the improvements as well as maximize the amount of quality time we would have to spend with them in the future.

Deliberation

While deliberating on what we could do and how, we concluded that we needed to at least do the following prior to making a final "selection'" regarding the situation at hand.

- We must agree among ourselves whether we truly wanted to commit a portion of our income to build and maintain a new house in Georgia.

It did not take us long to come to the conclusion that the investment would not only be good for Mom and Dad but would also provide a potential tax write-off against future income. In addition, it would eliminate the need for us and others to reserve hotel rooms during our visits to Vienna.

- We had to determine how to convince Earl's parents to allow us to build the house for them. Mrs. Carrie Bell had previously stated many times that she did not want any of her children spending money on them. She was adamant about not wanting to hear her children "fussing" over who did what for them.

  We were able to convince Earl's parents by assuring them that we "both" felt strongly about building the new house. We also were able to convince them that it would not be a burden on us since we both were gainfully employed and had promising careers. We promised that we would address any family issues upfront by speaking with all of Earl's sisters and brothers to get their approval and support.

- We had to actually obtain Earl's siblings approval and support for the idea.

  We started with Earl's oldest sister Laura. Her long-time husband, Alex, had died of prostate cancer a few years earlier. She expressed the possibility of her being in a position to relocate back to Georgia in the near future. She marveled at the idea of having a new house in Vienna. The improved living conditions would aid in her efforts to be able to care for Mom and Dad at home in their later years. Earl's conversations with Doris, Artice Jr., Andrew, Gloria, Selma and Alfonso also were extremely positive. They all were in varying stages of raising families and were not in the position themselves to take an equity stake in the project. However, they all indicated that they would help wherever they could.

- Then, we had to develop a plan for getting the job done while both of us were at the peak of our careers and living 2000 miles from the construction site.

  This was most challenging. We agreed that it was important to select a good local construction contractor that we could trust. We both also felt that is was important that we share the undertaking with our respective managers at work so that they would understand why we might have to take a number of three-day weekends over the next few months to fly down to the work site for periodic inspections.

Selection

After reviewing the financial arrangements, investigating the possibility of obtaining a local building contractor to perform the work and completing all discussions with Earl's parents & siblings, we selected a response to this circumstance. We decided to move forward with a project to build Mom and Dad a new house in Georgia. We named the undertaking, *Project Love.*

Our response was based on our belief that a new house was what was needed based the condition at hand. In addition, we believed that its utility would enrich the lives of our entire family. A new Cobb home would not only become a place for the Cobb family and friends to frequently gather and maintain loving relationships but would also provide a more comfortable and safer place for Mom and Dad to live. Moreover, it could possibly extend the amount of time we would have to enjoy them.

Engagement

New house being constructed on home site

Once we had decided to move forward with the project, we knew that a focused engagement effort was critical. Just as important was the need for us to take action quickly to establish momentum.

We developed a plan to build the new home on the same lot where the existing

37

home was located. This would allow Mom and Dad to remain in their old house while the new house was being constructed. This arrangement was essential. It was also a determining factor to getting Mom and Dad to agree with the new home construction.

Earl finalized Mom and Dad's approval to proceed with the new home construction by getting them to deed the land over to us. We worked with a local attorney to make sure the property lines were surveyed and accurately recorded in the Dooly County records. The attorney had known Artice and Carrie Bell for years. His initial concern was that we might not live up to this undertaking and leave Mom and Dad out in the cold. But, once he was briefed on the plans and sensed our level of commitment, his concerns quickly subsided. The deed transfer was necessary to enable the mortgage financing. It also ensured that the value of the property improvement would not impact Mom and Dad's Social Security and Medicare --- their only source of retirement income and medical coverage.

We then established a banking relationship with the local bank in Vienna and opened a joint checking account with Mom and Dad. The account would initially be used to retain the funds required for landscaping expenses and to pay Mortgage closing costs. The account would be replenished on a monthly basis to provide funds to cover property taxes and home maintenance expenses.

Over the following months, we began to execute a long list of activities which included the following:

• We identified and hired a reputable, local building contractor.

This was not an easy chore. We eventually had to travel to Dublin, a Georgia town about 80 miles from Vienna, to find a contractor we felt comfortable with and could trust to build the new family home.

• We developed the home construction plans and obtained the zoning and building permits.

We shared all of the home plans with Earl's parents as they were being drafted. Mom and Dad both were involved in making final decisions on kitchen design, flooring, closets and light fixtures. They really enjoyed being involved in the decision making process. It was great to see the renewed energy in both Mom and Dad. It appeared that just the idea of getting a new house had already began to add years onto their lives.

- We obtained local financing for a new home mortgage.

- We managed the three month construction project while living in Arizona, some 2,000 miles from the construction site.

- We performed periodic construction inspections and eventually a final walk through prior to accepting the finished product.

- We developed a plan, along with Earl's sisters and brothers, to move Mom and Dad into their new home.

Home site prior to moving old house

However, one item we had to carefully address was how to remove the old house from the site. We all knew that this would be an emotional transition for Mom and Dad. The old house was more than a house. It was the place that Dad had built with his own hands. It was the place where Mom and Dad had raised their family together and where they had lived for over 40 years.

As it turned out, it was Mrs. Carrie who became aware of a federal housing program that eventually would agree to accept and pay to move the old house. I recall Mom calling Earl in his office at Motorola one afternoon. Earl said that she seem so excited. She could not wait to share that she had identified a method by wish she would

39

save us the cost of moving the old house. More importantly, she was ecstatic that the plan would not require that the old house be demolished.

Outcomes

Construction of the new house and the new Cobb home was completed in January 1993. With the help of their daughters, Mom and Dad moved into the new home later that month.

It is an 1,800 sq. ft., four bedroom, ranch-style house with central air conditioning and heating. The master bedroom is equipped with bathroom hand rails and other fixtures that Mom and Dad would need as they became less mobile. All three guest bedrooms are on the south end of

Artice and Carrie Bell Cobb in Front of Their new house in Vienna

the house. This was to accommodate the visiting family members and to provide Mom and Dad their needed privacy. The backyard features a custom deck built around a huge pecan tree that had been on the family lot for nearly 60 years.

A new house for Mom and Dad

We were able to donate the old house to the Federal Housing program. The program paid to move the old house to a new home site. The program remodeled the house, added a small porch and made it available to a low income family in the local area.

The old house is now located just nine miles away from the original home site. Mom was very pleased to see the old house still providing a home for another happy family. Over the next two decades, the new Cobb home would host many family re-unions and celebrations --- including Mom and Dad's 71st wedding Anniversary

Mrs. Carrie Bell was a great cook and she thoroughly enjoyed her new kitchen. Everyone in Vienna were sure to attend the Saint Mark Baptist Church's "Big Meetings" (the local vernacular for major church events such as anniversaries) to get their hands on Mom's pineapple layer cakes and pecan pies. She lived to see her 87th birthday before peacefully being called to her heavenly home on June 29, 2009 after a lengthy bout with Alzheimer's disease.

Earl's Dad, now age 93, and his oldest sister, Laura, are presently living in the "new" house. The house is still the Cobb family's home and the family gathering place for special occasions.

Most of the Cobb Family during 1993 family reunion

Thoughts Regarding Our Exploration

The time we spent together working on *Project Love* in the early 1990's contributed to strengthening our marriage and enriching our life. Our confidence in our career success and our desire to maintain, leverage and strengthen family relationships were significant factors in guiding our mind-set during this period of our life.

Being comfortable with who we were as individuals and as a couple, allowed us to emotionally recognize and accept the challenges associated with shaping the outcome of this circumstance such that we could seize the enrichment opportunities.

A deeper understanding of our decision making tendencies and what we valued in personal relationships during this time in our life allowed us to come to the conclusion that the circumstance we were faced did not only encompass the well-being of Earls' parents. It also encompassed the love we had for each other, our mutual need for family closeness and the personal benefit we both gain from sharing our financial gifts with family and friends. In addition, and certainly without prior intent, by initiating and following through with *Project Love*, we inched closer to shaping a part of the legacy we would leave with generations of family members to come.

Being aware of the importance of the internal and external factors in our life and having the wherewithal to make a decision that would continue to enrich our life for decades into the future generated a different view of our life together. We began to see life, not simply as a collection of random events but as a continuum of opportunity for growth and life enrichment.

STAYING IN OUR DAUGHTER'S LIFE

MODAL EXPLORATION

Discovery

On a warm May morning in 1987 Charlotte and I were having a

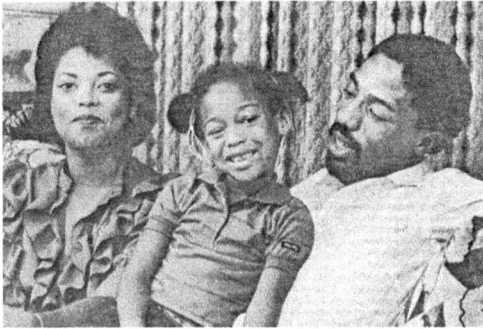

Earl and Charlotte relax in their Tempe, Arizona home
with Brandi, Age 5, in 1982

long discussion while enjoying a cup of Starbuck's coffee in the kitchen of our home in Mill Creek, Washington. The topic centered on whether or not we should relocate back to the Phoenix area. I had just received an offer to return to Motorola as a senior program manager. I had already tentatively accepted the offer extended to me by the division general manager and long-time mentor. However, knowing my overall situation at the time, he gave me a week or so to make the final decision.

We had moved to the Seattle area in July of 1986. Charlotte had completed her MBA at Arizona State University. Shortly after graduation she was offered the opportunity to become a stockbroker with a well-known investment firm. She had been heavily recruited by the company. However, we had to relocate to accept a position in their Seattle office. We both

43

agreed that it was an excellent opportunity for her and one that we should take full advantage.

Conversely, leaving the Phoenix area required that I leave my management position and the ten years I had invested in my career with Motorola. I was fortunate and quickly landed an opportunity to become the Manager of Program Management with the Power Conversion Division of ELDEC, a mid-market company located in Mill Creek, a Seattle suburb.

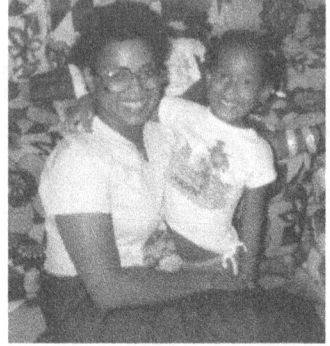

Brandi and Charlotte enjoy a playful moment in 1981

Prior to deciding to leave Phoenix in 1986, I had reached an agreement with my ex-wife, Angela, regarding how we were to maintain joint custody of our daughter, Brandi Renee. Brandi was turning nine later that year and was eager to move into her third year of school. The agreement would allow Charlotte and me to enroll Brandi in a Seattle school that fall.

Angela and I had agreed on a shared custody arrangement as a part of our divorce decree in 1981. The agreement allowed Brandi to spend six months of the year with each parent. We had successfully maintained an amiable relationship regarding our daughter and her well-being since our initial separation in 1979. Angela and I both agreed that I was in a better station in life, at the time, to provide for the education of our daughter.

Brandi was four years old when Charlotte and I were married in 1982. She was in our wedding and had always been a part of our family. Shortly after we settled in Seattle in July 1986, we began discussing with Angela the logistics around Brandi's move to Seattle. However, in September of 1986, Angela surprisingly shared with us that she had changed her mind. She was planning to keep our daughter in Phoenix.

Charlotte and I both were around thirty years old at the time. We were quite mature for our age and were comfortable with our personal and professional lives. Yet, Angela's decision produced an unexpected and emotionally significant event in our life. Quite frankly, it spun the first jointly shared set of potentially life altering circumstances we had experienced since we were married. We quickly realized that the choice of our initial response to the most pressing circumstance was quite binary. We could either remain in Seattle, a place we had really come to love and to call our new home *without* our daughter or return to Phoenix and forge a means to stay in our daughter's life during her most formative years.

During our initial evaluation of our dilemma, we discovered several circumstances that had to be addressed as well as potential opportunities to enrich our lives. Among the circumstances was the need to orchestrate another major move in less than a couple of years and the requirement to navigate the uncertainty of another career change for both of us. Of the potential opportunities, the one that stood out as most promising was the possible lifelong benefits that could be gained from being in a position to have a positive influence on our daughter and her life. Being closer to her geographically would mean being available to provide the moral, spiritual and additional financial support she would need on a consistent basis. After much thought and discussion, we concluded the following:

Charlotte hugs Brandi at her Wedding in 1982. Brandi was the Ring Bearer.

Our Circumstance: It would be easier for us to *simply accept* this unilateral change in plan as the response to our circumstance.

45

However, we knew that with this response, *the circumstance* itself would continue to dictate how and when we would be involved in our daughter's life. In addition, we would have to live the rest of our life not knowing how things might have been different if we had placed ourselves in a position to be closer to our daughter and in her life on a daily basis. On the contrary, we knew that we could not simply just move back to Phoenix. We must also be willing and capable of taking whatever actions that would be necessary to remain in our daughter's life in a meaningful way.

Our Opportunity: As stated above, being closer to Brandi geographically would mean being available to provide what she would need on a consistent basis. On the other hand, we both understood that there was no guarantee that being physically closer to our daughter would result in her meeting our expectations or ensure that her life would be one of achievement. There was also no way of knowing what she would add to or take away from our life. Nonetheless, we believed that our lives would be enriched by the opportunity to have a constructive and engaging place in our daughter's life. We also felt strongly that we needed to cultivate a relationship with Brandi that would be significant and long lasting.

Deliberation

During our deliberation, we compiled a list of things we needed to more closely examine and thoroughly understand. The list of items focused around Angela's decision to keep Brandi in Phoenix and how we would manage a successful relocation back to Phoenix. We knew that we had to carefully construct a transition that would support our ultimate objective.

Our final list included the following:

- We had to determine if there was the possibility that Angela would eventually have a change of mind (and heart) and move forward with what we believed was the original agreement of allowing Brandi to be enrolled in the Seattle school system.

In subsequent discussions with Angela, I learned that she was steadfast in her decision not to honor her earlier agreement. I also sensed that her decision was slanted more toward the child support payments versus a genuine concern with Brandi's education. Per the divorce decree, Angela would not receive the several hundred dollars of monthly child support payments during the time Brandi was not staying with her.

- We had to investigate the possibility of Charlotte not having to resign her position with Dean Witter Reynolds by transferring to another position within the company in the Phoenix area.

After several weeks of pursuing this possibility, Charlotte finally received her answer regarding the transfer request. Although the idea was intriguing and supported by her immediate supervisor, there were no immediate transfer opportunities in Phoenix at that time. This unearthed another circumstance that we would have to address. Charlotte would now have to seek a new position with another financial services company upon our return to Phoenix.

Brandi dressed in school uniform at age six

- I needed to negotiate a final offer with Motorola that would help defray the moving and relocation expenses. We anticipated that we would have to quickly get settled back in Phoenix in order to immediately initiate a new job search for Charlotte. We also needed to initiate our efforts to get our daughter enrolled in a good school close to our new home that fall.

I was able to present a good case as to the value I would bring to Motorola and the program management position. My relationship with Motorola management, the timing and the need to fill the position with experience, resulted in me obtaining an excellent relocation package, including a cash bonus. The generous relocation package would support our need to complete a timely transition and financially support our efforts to stay in our daughter's life.

- We had to construct a plan. The plan would need to be one that we were capable and willing to execute. We knew that, at a minimum, we would have to maintain the six-month custody arrangement established in the 1981 divorce decree. However, we felt that due to the unexpected adversarial relationship that was developing between us and Brandi's mother, it may be necessary to pursue an extended custody arrangement in order to provide the environment that our daughter would need to truly benefit from our return.

  We would have to prepare ourselves both financially and emotionally to make sure that we were in a position to seize this opportunity. It would be important that we were also in a position to shape a positive outcome to this unexpected event for our daughter as well as ourselves. We both were well aware that this ordeal would test the strength of our marriage and our resolve.

Selection

Following what seemed to us to be a thorough and successful period of deliberation, I accepted Motorola's offer to return to Phoenix. We both resigned our positions with two wonderful companies and prepared ourselves for our mission to stay in our daughter's life.

We selected a course of action which, in our minds, provided us a reasonable chance to seize the opportunity at hand. The deliberate response we selected to address the circumstances surrounding this major event in our life was developed by evaluating a multitude of factors. However, both of us had agreed that the primary reason to make another move at this time was to put ourselves in the best position to cultivate a relationship with our daughter that would be significant and long lasting. We also wanted to never to be in the position of wondering *what might have been different* in all of our lives if we had not made a move at this time. We coined this episode in our life, *Project Hope.*

Engagement

We completed our return to the Phoenix area in July of 1987. I immediately started my new position with Motorola's Government and Systems Technology Group in Scottsdale.

Charlotte quickly initiated her search for a new job. Based on the downturn in the stock market and the brokerage business in 1987, she decided to pursue a position in banking. To our good fortune, Charlotte secured a position with Citibank Arizona (which subsequently became Norwest Bank and then Wells Fargo Bank). She started as an institutional trust portfolio manager.

Brandi following family vacation to Hawaii to celebrate her 16[th]Birthday

Over the next ten years, we would add to and build upon proactive and reactive episodes associated with *Project Hope.* We would also witness an unexpected and significant growth in our personal strength, our professional achievements and our financial worth --- all as an offshoot of our decision to return to Phoenix and to stay in our daughter's life.

Some of the most memorable activities and outcomes associated with our undertaking to stay in our daughter's life during her formative years included the following:

- Purchasing a new home in north Scottsdale and getting Brandi enrolled in the fourth grade in the Scottsdale Unified School System.

- Hiring an attorney to represent us in a renewed child custody battle spurred on by Brandi's mother's decision and legal action to gain full custody.

- Securing the services of a clinical psychologist to aid in determining the family environment that would best support both the psychological and educational development of our daughter.

- Reaching an agreement which provided us with legal custody of our daughter for nine months of the year along with Brandi spending the summers with her mother. We agreed to pay Angela the monthly child support even during the months that Brandi lived with us.

- Enrolling Brandi in a new middle school in Scottsdale and providing Brandi with tutorial services to support and strengthen her math and science skills.

- Enrolling Brandi in a Scottsdale Boys and Girls Clubs after school program. Brandi also worked as a volunteer and won an outstanding achievement award.

- Taking a family trip during school break to Hawaii to celebrate Brandi's 16th birthday.

- Enrolling Brandi in High School in Scottsdale and providing support of her interest in theater.

- Planning and taking trips with Brandi to several colleges and universities, including Tennessee State, Spelman and Clark-Atlanta, to explore potential interest.

- Responding to challenges of Brandi's adolescence and her rejection of our values and accomplishment-oriented lifestyle.

50

- Eventually agreeing to Brandi's constant request to move back in with her mother during her junior year in high school and withdrawing from a quality Scottsdale School system.

Outcomes

As we mentioned earlier, going into *Project Hope,* Charlotte and I both were well aware that the ordeal would most likely test the strength of our marriage and our resolve.

In hindsight, our analysis of the actual outcomes and subsequent events associated with *Project Hope* reminded us of a quote attributed to Sasha Azevedo, an American actress, athlete and model. She was once asked about how she faces life's challenges. She responded with the following:

"I do believe that when we face challenges in life that are far beyond our own power, it's an opportunity to build on our faith, inner strength, and courage. I've learned that how we face challenges plays a big role in the outcome of them."

We believe that we faced the challenges associated with our sincere efforts to cultivate a significant and long lasting relationship with our daughter with *faith, strength* and *courage.* We also took into the undertaking realistic expectations and a commitment to effectively manage, in parallel, all of the other aspects of our life.

During the same period of our life which was consumed by *Project Hope,* our personal, professional and community life flourished as a result of us encountering and successfully responding to new events and circumstances.

Charlotte survived multiple bank mergers and became a vice president with Norwest Bank where she headed a large corporate trust portfolio. I received

Earl (standing far left) was one of the seven African-American Vice Presidents in all of Motorola, Inc. in 1995

several promotions within Motorola and assumed executive responsibilities for large business activities. In 1993, I became a group vice president, traveled extensively internationally and later headed Motorola's world-wide military radio systems business. Charlotte and I both were on multiple Boards of Phoenix area civic and community organizations. We finally were able to spend some quality time with Charlotte's parents who had moved from their family home in Alaska to their retirement home in Colorado Springs. We even took on another Project and built my parents a new house down in middle Georgia.

Charlotte's Parents, Alberta and Julius Grant - Following their move to Colorado Springs.

Even with all of the other demands placed on us we still dedicated quality time and made a concentrated effort to have an engaging relationship with our daughter.

However, as Brandi struggled with adolescence, we struggled with penetrating a *mental wall* that Brandi seemed to have established between her and us. It appeared then, as it does now, that this *wall* is constructed to separate, in her mind, the two fundamentally different lifestyles tugging for her affection.

As a result, the *Project Hope* engagement period turned out to be one of the *most rewarding*, yet one of the *most disappointing* decades of our life together.

Thoughts Regarding Our Exploration

Nonetheless, as we reflect back on our efforts to not only stay in our daughter's life but to become an engaging and influential force, we can see how we succeeded on several fronts.

We will never have to wonder *what might have been different* in all of our lives if we had *not* decided, in 1987, to relocate back to Phoenix. We were there, we gave it our best and we, in hindsight, became better individuals and a closer couple as a result of *responding* versus simply *reacting* to this life altering circumstance.

Brandi, age 21, during a visit to our Ohio home in 1998

As we recall, our initial thoughts were to *react* to Angela's decision by shutting down and just saying *"the heck with it"*. We, for a brief moment, might have thought that our life would have been better during that time if all we had to do was send a check every month and pay for a plane ticket to visit with Brandi during the holidays and school breaks. However, we were aware that it was not the major events in our life that had necessarily determined our life's outcomes. We knew that, to the contrary, many outcomes were dependent upon how well we responded to the resulting circumstances. Our response to this circumstance required us to take the time, dedicate the resources and use our natural gifts to shape the best outcome.

Because we believed that life was more than simply a collection of random events, we allowed the other facets in our life [i.e. careers, relationships, education, goals, etc.] to continue to take their course as we still maintained focus on our daughter and the relationship we believed would enrich all three of our lives.

Even with all of the *twists and turns* taken during *Project Hope*, we still love and we are proud of our daughter.

We are also just as proud of the three beautiful and vastly different grandchildren she has brought into this world and into our life. We know that it was our *responses* to a number of difficult circumstances during *Project Hope* that laid the path for all six of us to be in a position to enjoy each other's earthly presence.

Just as we have hope for a richer life for our grandchildren, we also continue to be in a hopeful relationship with our daughter.

We all should be reminded from time to time of the words of George Elliott, *"It is never too late to be what you might have been".*

BECOMING A FRANCHISE OWNER

MODAL EXPLORATION

Discovery

In September of 1999, Charlotte and I had just returned from an eight day Caribbean cruise. We were in the process of relocating

Charlotte and Earl on cruise ship in 1999

from our home in Butler Township, just North of Dayton, Ohio, to a new home we were in the process of purchasing in an area known as Lake Norman, North Carolina. Lake Norman was a new and growing suburb about 15 miles north of Charlotte NC.

The inviting Lake Norman community had evolved over a 60 year period with homes eventually peppering a 450 mile man-made lake which was master planned as a part of a Duke Energy nuclear power plant.

The relocation was the result of my corporate vice president position with the Reynolds and Reynolds Company being eliminated following the sale of the company's Healthcare Systems Division. We made the decision not to remain in the Dayton area in the summer of 1999.

Based on an ongoing economic recession and the challenges in the job market, we were leaning toward pursuing an entrepreneurial lifestyle. We had visited a close friend, Clement Ashford, in Charlotte North Carolina several months

The Cobb's Lake Norman home in 1999

earlier. We immediately fell in love with Lake Norman. We were fortunate to find a beautiful home in a quiet cove known as Sterling Point just off of Interstate 77 and Highway 77. The 3,000 sq. ft. ranch style home was on the lake and included a private boat slip located only a short distance from our back yard. We would later purchase a 24-foot Harris Kayot pontoon cruiser and enjoy entertaining friends with sight-seeing tours of the vast lake and tranquil environment. The new house and the freshness of the Charlotte, NC region appeared to be just perfect for the next phase of our life.

As a part of our move to Dayton in 1997, Charlotte had decided to not seek new employment and to take a sabbatical to

pursue a second post graduate degree. In 1999, Charlotte completed the course work and began work on her dissertation. She would soon receive a well-earned professional Doctorate Degree in Nutrition Counseling from LaSalle University.

Earl, Charlotte and Friend Marty onboard the Cobb's pontoon cruiser named "MI"

We actually began our discussions regarding Charlotte's return to the workforce when we first arrived in Dayton. A nutrition-based retail business and the category of customers it would attract would complement the nutritional consulting and coaching practice she had planned to launch after graduation. Following the Reynolds and Reynolds experience and the need now to move quickly toward new sources of income, we began to more seriously consider an investment in a national retail franchise to make this idea a reality.

After returning from vacation in mid-September, we began to more aggressively research the nutrition products industry. We were most interested in identifying the best franchising opportunities. Through her research, Charlotte determined that the top rated company, General Nutrition Centers or GNC, was offering new franchises in the United States and that a Charlotte, NC location was a possibility. GNC appeared to have a unique business model. It had developed both company-owned and franchised outlets in comparable numbers. We decided to pursue the idea of becoming GNC owner/operators. After completing the necessary applications and other documents we continued to further investigate the company and its franchise format. Several weeks into the process, we learned that we had been pre-qualified as a potential franchisee.

Thus, by December 1999, it was appearing as if the "stars were lining up" for us to move to Charlotte, NC and purchase a GNC franchise as our first entry into a new entrepreneurial lifestyle. We were both excited about the idea. We could afford the franchise fee and investment required. We liked the Charlotte, NC market and the franchisor seemed to be offering a proven and successful business format.

However, we had to factor into our decision the fact that even though I had obtained an excellent severance package from Reynolds and Reynolds, becoming entrepreneurs at this stage in life (we were both in our mid-forties) may not support the corporate life style of which we had become accustomed.

Our Circumstance: After 25 years, we found ourselves in a dilemma, where due to corporate downsizing neither of us was employed. Yet, we had become accustomed to a corporate lifestyle and income level. The most pressing circumstance spun by this potential life altering event was the need to replace our income source --- preferably with the opportunity that matched our current experience and aspirations.

We needed to decide whether to primarily focus on finding new corporate jobs, in a challenging employment environment of the late 1990's or pursue other alternatives. Of course, the most likely option at this stage of life would be to leverage our extensive business training and experience in some entrepreneurial capacity.

Our Opportunity: To take advantage of the wealth we had accumulated and the timing of this unexpected transition, we should respond to our genuine desire to enter the world of entrepreneurship and possible financial independence. Even though we would risk not being able to replace our previous income levels, we both valued and were passionate about the possibility of utilizing our business development skills and potentially establishing a successful business.

We envisioned the initial business success leading to the establishment of a viable, long term family-owned enterprise. We often talked about establishing such an enterprise which would be available for our daughter, grandchildren, nieces and nephews to leverage as a starting point and possible employment fallback as they worked to carve out the next generation of livelihoods for themselves and their families.

Deliberation

During our deliberation, we thought it would be prudent to more closely analyze both the circumstance in which we found ourselves and the "pros and cons" associated with moving too quickly into starting our own business. Consequently, we

58

compiled two separate lists. Each list outlined what we needed to consider more thoroughly prior to selecting a response to the circumstance at hand.

Regarding the circumstance, we outlined the two key areas we felt we should more thoroughly explore.

- We should develop a household budget to determine how long we could sustain ourselves at the current lifestyle until we needed to supplement our monthly cash flow with new income.

  Since we had always maintained a monthly household budget and were fortunate to have been in a position for a number of years to not have to accumulate any major credit card or consumer debt, we were able to rather quickly determine that, by prudently stretching the monthly severance payments, we could sustain ourselves for 12 to 18 months.

- We should make an assessment of whether or not one or both of us should pursue a new corporate position and the potential negative impact on future corporate opportunities, for either or both of us, if we were out of the corporate work force for a substantial period of time.

  With Charlotte having left the corporate workforce in 1997 when we moved from Scottsdale to Dayton, she was already a couple of years removed from her banking career and the corporate work force. The probability for her returning anywhere similar to the level and pay grade that she vacated in a banking environment that was rapidly consolidating seemed remote. Furthermore, it would be her knowledge of nutrition and retail that would be needed to strategically plan the start-up of a new GNC franchise.

  Since I was part of a group of senior managers who had been displaced and were viewed as "casualties of the dot-com shake out" during the national recession of the late 1990's, I felt that

I should have the opportunity to get back into a comparable position within 6 to 8 months.

However, the technical management position for which I would be best suited most likely would not be found in the Charlotte, NC region. Based on the fact that it would take months before we would open a new GNC franchise in North Carolina and that it would be Charlotte who would oversee most of the day-to-day operation, it made sense for me to leverage my multi-industry background and pursue a new corporate position as soon as possible.

My successful tenures with some well-respected companies like Motorola and Reynolds and Reynolds should serve me well. On the other hand, if I am out of the executive pace for too long, it would become increasingly difficult to land a comparable position without some serious re-invention.

In terms of the "pros and cons" associated with moving too quickly into starting our own business, we compiled the following list of areas that we felt required further consideration:

- We should perform a significant amount of due diligence to ensure the viability of General Nutrition Center franchises and the quality of GNC's training and support for new franchisees.

    We actually began our due diligence of GNC several months prior to deciding to move to Charlotte. At the time, GNC was one of the largest and most popular franchisors in the world. The company had opened over 4,000 stores in the United States and over 1,200 franchise operations in 52 international markets. For nearly 75 years, GNC had been building a global reputation as the largest specialty retailer of nutritional products. We spoke with several current franchise owner/operators regarding their overall experience with the company, the products, the marketing strategies and the support they obtained from the corporate office. We also inquired about their actual financial performance vs. their initial expectations. The vast majority of the owner/operators we spoke with were quite pleased with their decision to become a GNC franchisee.

- We should understand the level of investment required and what to expect in terms of net income and profitability.

  We visited the GNC corporate office in Pittsburg, Pennsylvania. We spent a full day gaining visibility into their franchise system and discussing historical performance of new stores. For a total investment of approximately $125,000 to $200,000, including about $80,000 of capital equipment, we could expect to retain 7 to 10% profit on an average of $600,000 of sales revenue per store. It became obvious that in order to generate a net income of over $100,000, we would have to invest in multiple stores over time.

- We should perform our own analysis of the Charlotte, NC market to understand how well existing stores were performing and the available new store locations.

  Based on a collection of data provided by GNC and our own visits to the major locations in the greater Charlotte area, we found the Charlotte, NC market to be slightly above average. Knowing that past performance is no guarantee of future performance, we still felt comfortable with the growing Charlotte region and the new store sites that were available. Our first choice was a site designed with a new store format that GNC had recently developed. The new "store-in-store" format included smaller 800 to 1,000 sq. ft. stores located inside large, upscale grocery retailers. Most of the grocery stores also included bank locations. Even though the average revenue was smaller in stores with this format, the safety of not being located in a strip mall and the convenience of being able to make cash deposits without leaving the location were all attractive features --- especially with Charlotte planning to spend quite a bit of time in the store and managing the operations.

Selection

After carefully weighing all of our options, we selected a two pronged response to this circumstance. We would move forward with purchasing our first GNC franchise with Charlotte initially operating it solo. In addition, I would aggressively search for a new corporate position. Thus, we dubbed this journey, *Project 2-Source.*

With the financial wherewithal to give ourselves the time needed to fully pursue both paths, we began by developing a detailed business plan for the GNC business and utilizing an executive search consultant provided by Reynolds and Reynolds.

Engagement

The executive search portion of the response to our most pressing circumstance was fairly straight forward. With the assistance of a New York based consultant, provided as a part of my severance package, an effective search could be executed smoothly. The process included the usual: the development of an updated resume, the sharpening of focus on the industries/companies to be pursued, daily networking with colleagues and waiting for the right opportunity to surface. We knew that finding a new corporate position in a challenging employment economy would take time.

Dr. Grant-Cobb in GNC

Based on the approach we were taking as a response to our circumstance, this would provide the opportunity for me to remain in North Carolina, at least initially, as we tackled the new challenge of establishing a new business in a new city.

As planned, Charlotte took the lead in our effort to become a franchise owner and operator. Over the next four years we would start a business, grow a business and eventually close a business. The following are the most memorable events and significant milestones we encountered.

- Following nine months of preparatory tasks and activities, CobbCare GNC opened in December 2000. The GNC corporate office could not finalize the lease agreement with our first selection of location. Typically, it was GNC's real estate department which selected physical store sites well in advance of a store opening. Then, GNC would either open a company store on the site or sublease the space to a franchisee. After months of waiting, we agreed to purchase a company-owned store located about three miles north of our initial site selection. The store was one of the first outlets built inside a regional, high-end grocery store. The monthly sales revenue of the existing location was about half of where it should have been for this size store. Charlotte and her new CobbCare GNC team would have to really work to get this location up to expectations.

  The activities leading to the grand opening required a significant amount of planning. Charlotte worked with the various GNC contacts to make it all happen on time and within budget. The activities included: negotiating and signing of a franchise agreement which specified the new "store-in-store" format; hiring the initial staff; attending a two-week, mandatory training class at the GNC corporate headquarters; working with GNC real estate to identify and select store location; finalizing the design and layout of the store; agreeing to a build-out schedule and planning the grand opening; acquiring the necessary point of sale processing services; developing the first 90 day marketing and advertising plan; placing the first order for start-up product inventories; stocking of store; preparing signage for grand opening and distributing grand opening advertising.

- By the spring of 2001, Charlotte had doubled the monthly sales revenue. She strategically integrated select third party products with the GNC standard products in support of diabetic and menopausal health. She attracted a loyal following of customers, including our pastor, his family and a large number of church members. She instituted

Charlotte and Friend Ginny during Grand Opening of General Nutrition Center

a value shoppers program which rewarded frequent shoppers. She sponsored local "strong men" contests and significantly increased her sales of sports products. To her surprise, Charlotte was approached by the marketing department of the local university to participate in a program where students would develop competitive marketing plans based on her store location and product mix. The unique collaboration with the university provided some significant marketing and advertising insights.

- However, as the performance of the store continued to *soar*, CobbCare GNC's relationship with its landlord began to *sour*. The grocery store landlord refused to honor its agreement with GNC corporate to terminate the sale of certain nutritional items in their grocery store.

Charlotte and Earl in their GNC new store

During the holidays in 2002, the grocery store manager consistently placed grocery products in front of our store and refused to honor the terms of our

64

lease agreement which prohibited such placement. We later learned the grocer was in the process of adding an in-store pharmacy and had targeted the space we were leasing to accommodate the addition.

- In the fall of 2003, after several attempts to get GNC corporate to enforce our lease agreement with the grocer, we had no choice other than to proceed with legal action. We quickly reached a settlement with GNC and the grocer. Based on our overall experience with the landlord and GNC corporate during the previous three years, we decided to accept a cash buyout versus opening CobbCare GNC at another Charlotte, NC location.

Outcomes

Our primary objective of establishing a new income source following my departure from Reynolds and Reynolds and our move to Charlotte, NC was accomplished on both fronts.

The CobbCare GNC business success proved that we had what it takes to truly be entrepreneurial and generate major income. During the three full years of operation, Charlotte grossed in the mid to high five figures in annual sales revenue. With the unfortunate settlement that led to the closing of CobbCare GNC, we recovered our initial investment and then some. In February of 2001, I accepted a position as COO with a venture-capital-backed IT start-up with a great salary and stock ownership. More importantly I earned the opportunity to lead the company as its CEO through the tail-end of the dot-com era.

By responding to a major circumstance in a manner which encompassed our aspirations as well as our immediate financial needs, we gained significantly more than another income source.

As we are reminded by the Chinese Proverb, *"Give a man a fish and you feed him for a day. Teach a man to fish and you feed him for a lifetime."*

Thoughts Regarding Our Exploration

Certainly by being prepared financially to *weather a storm* as significant as major income loss was of tremendous value to us. On the other hand, as we reflect back on this event in our life, it becomes obvious that just as important as having had financial reserves was our ability to recognize all of our gifts (natural and acquired) and how we could leverage them to shape positive outcomes to major circumstances.

We lived in the Charlotte, NC area for a total of six years. During this time, in addition to addressing the challenges associated with *Project 2-Source*, we found the time to build many long lasting friendships. We were pleasantly surprised with the genuineness and helpfulness of both the professional and personal relationships we established. We found all of our acquaintances to be good people with plenty of goodwill.

Unlike many of the places we have lived, while in the Charlotte area, we made it a point to get out and explore the Carolinas --- from the piedmont to the coast. From Ashville to Raleigh and from Hilton Head to Myrtle Beach, we thoroughly enjoyed the sightseeing, golf, local cuisine, conversation and the precious time we spent together. Our decision to respond to the circumstance which surfaced as a result of a shorter stay in Ohio than we expected, not only added to our confidence of being able to earn a living outside of corporate America but also contributed significantly to the overall richness in our life.

Because we were aware of who we were at this time as a couple and what was important to us, we mustered the courage to shape an outcome which had dimensions of richness far beyond just replacing an income source.

JOINING THE BETTERLIVING™ FAMILY

MODAL EXPLORATION

Discovery

The spring of 2004 was a time of personal reflection and professional frustration for both of us. Earl, as the CEO of Maryland-based MedContrax, had completed the unrewarding chore of leading the company into a strategic alignment with an industry rival. The asset merger was necessitated by MedContrax's inability to close a second round of venture capital funding following the September 11, 2001 terrorist attack.

Cobb's home at Harroway
at the Lakes in 2004

He had returned back to our home in Charlotte, NC later that year. He was currently working as an executive consultant for a Charlotte-based management consulting firm as well as working as an adjunct professor of management at DeVry University's Keller Graduate School of Management.

We had sold our General Nutrition Center (GNC) franchise in the fall of 2003. Due to a sublease issue with the franchisor, we agreed to a legal settlement which allowed us to sell the franchise back to GNC at a premium. However, the primary disappointment of the entire GNC experience was our relationship as a franchisee with the GNC corporate office. The company had recently been purchased by a new ownership group. The ownership change seemed to also bring a change of management philosophy. GNC corporate managers appeared to no longer be as supportive of their 2000 franchise locations as they were of their 2000 corporate owned stores. From competing pricing to conflicting information regarding product shelf life, the list of issues [being experienced by many GNC franchise owner/operators] grew to the point where we realized that maintaining the relationship with GNC as a franchisee was not in our best interest.

During this time, I was doing freelance work as a part of our CobbCare Consulting business. We had sold the lake house a year earlier and had purchased another wonderful home in the Lake Norman area not far from the old Sterling Point location. The new house was in a development known as Harroway at the Lakes. With over 3,000 sq. ft. of living space, we each had home offices on the second floor and managed to coexist peacefully as we logged long workdays.

Even though we were busy and financially stable, we both felt that we were not fully utilizing our talents and still had an "itch" to be CEOs of our own company.

Following a visit to North Carolina by our daughter, Brandi, and her first child early in 2004, we began to more seriously discuss why we felt the need to get involved in another business start-up at this time. Initially, we admitted to ourselves that our situation had the makings of a true *conundrum*. But, after several weeks of back-and-forth dialogue, we began to analyze the situation more thoroughly. We wanted to finally get our minds around what was driving us to desire another entrepreneurial episode in our life.

For me, I concluded that through the CobbCare GNC experience, I had demonstrated that I had what it takes to generate and execute a marketing plan and drive the operations of a business to consistent profitability. But, more importantly, through the experience, I found that growing a small business which completely embodied my own values and personality was much more satisfying than many of the multi-million dollar deals I was involved in during my investment banking days.

Earl mostly talked about how immensely he enjoyed his leadership position with MedContrax and was intrigued by the contrast it provided as compared to his extensive experience in leading major businesses within Fortune 500 companies. We had just celebrated his 50th birthday --- a celebration which included a James Bond themed party I hosted at our home and attended by over fifty friends, family members and well-wishers --- and was becoming more and more anxious about the window of time available to him to build upon his venture experience.

It seemed that both of us, particularly after Brandi's visit, were beginning to feel more strongly about addressing our need to take another *shot* at establishing a family enterprise. It was our long time goal to eventually establish a viable business which would be available for our daughter and grandchildren to leverage as they carved out the next generation of livelihoods for themselves and their families.

As a consequence of this situational analysis, we surprisingly found that multiple events in our lives over the past several years [most resulting in positive outcomes] had generated an undeniable circumstance which had surfaced at this time in our life.

Our Circumstance: Although we find ourselves busy and financially stable, we are still driven to respond to an intense desire to get involved in another business start-up. Our desire seems to encompass a combination of being at a stage in life where we are not fully utilizing our extensive business development experience and an acute sensation almost certainly caused by having been bitten again by the "entrepreneurial bug". Since we are both around 50 years old, we would probably also be deciding whether or not we would ever again get involved in a significant new business startup.

Our Opportunity: If we decide to get involved in another business startup at this time, we could set the company's growth on a trajectory such that we could target retirement and getting young family members involved in the business within the next ten years. The idea of establishing an enterprise which would be available for our daughter, grandchildren, nieces and nephews to leverage in support of their livelihoods has been a long time goal. With the financial resources, good health and burning desire currently available to invest in the right business --- now might be our *best shot* at succeeding and reaching this goal.

Deliberation

Prior to selecting the appropriate response to our circumstance, we must first determine how we would select and assess a business which would generate significant annual revenue and have the potential to appreciate in value in the long term. Because of the magnitude of the financial investment that would be required, we felt that we should spend the time upfront to clearly understand the most critical aspects of such a business venture. After considerable deliberation, we concluded that the following three areas encompassed those aspects:

• We should outline the attributes of the type of business which would best provide us with what we would enjoy doing on a daily basis, the level of challenge we required and a means of achieving our longer term expectations.

Earl and I both agreed that our next business enterprise must have three key attributes.

70

The first was that the business must have the potential to generate three to five million dollars of annual revenue. This level of sales revenue was important. Within this range we could expect to net a five figure income and still have assets to invest in and grow the business. Most likely this would rule out a typical consulting type start-up which would be limited to the number of hours we could work. It would probably require that we either deliver a large volume of low-to-moderate priced products/services on an annual basis or ship a smaller number of higher priced items.

Secondly, the business must complement our combination of skills and interests. I would be most interested in a business which required a lot of customer touch and provided products and/or services which could, to some degree, be customized to meet the customer's individual needs. I also would enjoy a good marketing and creative advertising challenge. I knew that Earl, with his technical and operations management background, would be most interested in developing product and/or service delivery strategies, designing operational processes and working directly with the customers to ensure their total satisfaction.

Thirdly, the business must be one in which the operating model requires it to build and retain a significant amount of equity or value over time. Having spent a number of years operating smaller businesses to this point, we both realized that the facts are such that you live off the cash flow and you retire by selling the business or leveraging the retained equity.

- We should develop a "short list" of potential business categories that possessed such attributes. Then, conduct an assessment of each to determine the best candidate at this time.

Prior to this point, we had owned and operated two rather significant-sized small businesses in the Charlotte, NC area. In addition to a General Nutrition Center franchise which provided a well-defined

71

operating format, we had also launched a business that we actually designed and built from "scratch" named Transit Express. Transit Express was a next-day and regional package delivery business that we opened in the spring of 2000 during the peak of the dot-com era. The sales were driven by major contracts with companies like Federal Express, Sears and Owens-Corning. Transit Express had a customer base of over 100 daily-use business customers across Mecklenburg County. After the business grew into an enterprise which included four company-owned 24/7 vans, a number of rental trucks, twelve employees and a warehouse, we sold the entire unit, as is, to a regional cargo logistics company based on an offer we could not refuse.

Therefore, along with the larger business units we had managed while in corporate America, we also had hands-on experience with smaller businesses with varying operating formats. Based on these experiences, we had a fairly good idea of the type of business that would meet our requirements for this new venture. So, we spent several weeks developing a list of potential business opportunities. Our research included working with business brokers, perusing the Wall Street Journal and other leading ad spots and surfing numerous websites. Generating the initial list was not much of a problem. However, getting this list down to what could be called a "short list" was the real challenge. We were leaning more toward businesses with a proven operating format, quality products/services and an excellent reputation based on customer referrals. We did not want another enterprise that we had to start from scratch. We had carved our list down to three real possibilities, but needed to make a final decision fairly quickly.

We finally decided, based on a trip to Souderton, Pennsylvania, that the best candidate possessing all of the attributes we had established and was within our "investment reach" was a Betterliving™ Patio and Sunrooms dealership being offered by a fifty year old company named Craft-Bilt Manufacturing.

Craft-Bilt was the leading sunroom manufacturer in the United States. The company also was the country's fastest growing manufacturer of awnings, canopies and solar shades. Other Craft-Bilt products included screen rooms, patio covers and fully engineered building panels. We were being offered a dealership which would cover 19 counties in the piedmont of North and South Carolina. Craft-Bilt's business model for their Betterliving™ dealerships was based on building high-quality, custom designed products at reasonable prices. Their sales and advertising strategy was fueled by targeted television infomercials. The Betterliving™ dealer sales, marketing and production training appeared to be among the best in the industry. Even though the strength of the patio and sunroom product was "construction", the heart of the business was marketing and sales. The average room sale could range from $15,000 to $40,000 and most customers brought their own financing via cash or home equity.

Thus, a Betterliving™ Patio and Sunrooms dealership appeared to meet all of the business attributes we required --- A marketing and sales driven, high quality, high ticket, low volume, skills-based, customer-oriented business with a protected territory large enough to build significant enterprise equity over time.

- We should develop a business plan which is realistic and capable of being executed within the investment and time limits we would establish.

This is where I turned to Earl and said "go for it". Earl had developed such a knack for thinking through and "operationalizing" business plans. When we first moved to the Charlotte, NC area he assisted me with the GNC franchise business plan. Of course, it was his plan that was the impetus behind Transit Express. He had also developed plans for several local groups in the region, ranging from aspiring entrepreneurs to seasoned business veterans.

Earl worked with Craft-Bilt Manufacturing's Director of Business Development to validate many of the assumptions surrounding every aspect of the business. Craft-Bilt provided typical cost-to-price ratios as well as the demographics around the customer base and average room sales. Since Earl would be the one to manage the operations/production end of the business, he spent a lot of time thinking through the cost of hiring and training a quality room construction staff. The plan would be to initially ramp up slowly. However, the plan must ensure that quality construction techniques and customer schedules were consistently maintained. Since I would be responsible for sales and marketing, I provided the required staffing plans and cost estimates in these areas.

After we reviewed the final version of the document and walked through several "what if" scenarios, we both felt that we had developed a realistic plan. We still had to convince ourselves that a Charlotte-based business could be executed as planned and whether or not we could reach and surpass "breakeven" with the level of investment we would be willing to put into the endeavor.

The two main questions that were still keeping us up at night were: Will a sufficient number of suitable houses in the Piedmont region of the Carolinas support a sunroom addition and would the television advertising dollars in the plan be sufficient to attract the number of leads we would need to build and maintain a sustainable volume of orders?

Selection

Following another visit to the Craft-Bilt Manufacturing facility in Pennsylvania and some very candid and open conversations with the company's President, we had to make a decision. Not just on Craft-Bilt, but whether or not we really wanted to respond to the circumstance we were facing by engaging in another business startup at this time. After taking a few days away from it all and enjoying a weekend in Myrtle Beach, we decided to give another business start-up a *shot*.

The selection was really based on a number of reasons. We were convinced that the Betterliving™ dealership was an excellent match for us at this stage of our life. We would bring a tremendous amount of business experience and passion to a business based on a model that was working for scores of other dealers across the United States. The relationship we were

Earl and Charlotte in a conference photo with other owners of Betterliving™ Patio and Sunroom dealerships in 2005

developing with Craft-Bilt the *company* and Craft-Bilt the *people* felt comfortable. However, deciding to *join the Betterliving™ family* really came down to us both feeling that now was the time to take a *shot* at succeeding and reaching a long time goal. We optimistically named this new business venture *Project Better-Future.*

Engagement

The spring of 2004 was spent negotiating the terms of the Betterliving™ dealership agreement with Craft-Bilt and finalizing our business plan. We began to execute our plan within weeks after executing the agreement. In August 2005, we held the grand opening of *Betterliving™ Patio and Sunrooms of Central Carolinas.* I concentrated on adapting the standard administrative, marketing and sales processes to our dealership. Earl focused most of his attention on hiring a skilled construction team, attending the required installation training and obtaining the vehicles & equipment we would need to launch operations.

75

The months leading up to the dealership opening were full of long days. It was during this period that we also unearthed the first of several significant surprises.

What follows is an outline of the most significant milestones, activities and decisions associated with *Project Better-Future*.

- Fortunately, at the time we signed our dealership agreement with Craft-Bilt there was not a dealership fee. However, we were responsible for all expenses associated with establishing the enterprise in the Carolinas. To finance the dealership, we estimated that we would need to invest around $100,000 to cover the initial cost of facilities, vehicles, tools, equipment, insurance, training and staffing. Beyond the initial investment, we were prepared to inject up to another $150,000 to support other capital requirements and to assist with cash flow during the ramp-up phase of the business.

- By opening the dealership in August, we accepted the risk of not having a longer summer sales period to aid in building a backlog of orders. Summer was the most active sales period for dealerships in the North and East. However, we felt that in the South the fall and even the early winter weather was still fairly pleasant. Thus, the constraints on outside construction were not as severe as in other parts of the country.

- Prior to the August 2005 grand opening, we completed a long list of milestones. To this day, we are not sure how we successfully accomplished so many critical and somewhat challenging activities in this timeframe. Among them were:

    o We worked with a local bank and credit union to establish the banking and line of credit relationships we would need to support the business operations.

o We worked with an insurance broker to purchase the compulsory levels of hazard and workers compensation insurance. We also worked with a health insurance company and purchased an affordable policy to cover all full time employees.

o We worked with the City of Charlotte and Mecklenburg County to secure the licenses and bonds required to operate a construction business in the region.

o With the assistance of Earl's brother Andrew, a retired HR executive, we developed and published a complete set of Human Resources, Employee Conduct and Company Benefits manuals.

o We advertised in the local paper and hired our first two skilled carpenters, one experienced sales person and an office manager/administrative assistant.

o We worked with a commercial real estate broker to identify a facility to launch our initial operations. The Craft-Bilt facility recommendations included a 1,000 to 2,000 sq. ft. showroom to display some completed products as well as a warehouse ranging from 4,000 to 5,000 sq. ft. to maintain vehicles and sunroom construction materials.

o We started a 12-week course to prepare both us to take the North and South Carolina Contractors Examination to become licensed contractors in the two states.

o We purchased a new sub-compact car for sales calls and two new Ford F-250 trucks. We equipped the trucks with ladder racks, tools boxes and the required aluminum brake. Earl purchased all of the construction tools and warehouse fixtures required to safely install the custom built sunrooms.

o Earl and the carpenters attended a two week training course at the Craft-Bilt facility in Pennsylvania to become certified in designing and building both the standard and vinyl version of the rooms. To Earl's surprise, he was selected as top in his class based on written exams and actual construction demonstrations that were a part of the intense training. All of the Betterliving™ patio and sunrooms were constructed on-site. They were engineered structures consisting of cut-to-order extruded aluminum along with custom glass, doors and window components.

o Both Earl and I attended the week long sales class at the Craft-Bilt facility along with our new sales person. A significant part of successfully installing a Betterliving™ sunroom was ensuring that the room design met both the homeowner's expectations as well as the engineered room installation specifications. In other words, all room designs were not suited for all home layouts. There was also the need for exact measurements and other design features such as building code requirements for all existing or new decks and concrete slab foundations. The sales person's product knowledge and installation measurement skills were all critical to these aspects of the room sales and design process.

• The most challenging and what turned out to be the most revealing set of activities were associated with the selection of an adequate facility from which to initially launch the Betterliving™ Patio and Sunrooms of Central Carolinas enterprise. As mentioned above, Craft-Bilt management had specific recommendations for its Betterliving™ dealerships. We spent several days touring prospective locations and facilities with the Craft-Bilt President prior to the August 2005 grand opening. Earl spent a week traveling to existing Betterliving™ Patio and Sunrooms locations in the mid-west. The most recent Betterliving™ dealer expansions had occurred in the Milwaukee and Chicago areas. He toured the facilities and discussed start-up strategy with the other Betterliving™ dealers.

- You might not call it a *sixth-sense* but neither Earl nor I felt comfortable with this aspect of the start-up. We both were very concerned about entering into a four or five year commercial lease for 5,000 to 6,000 sq. ft. of office, showroom and warehouse space. We felt that we needed a better sense of how the Betterliving™ business model would work in the Carolinas market prior to making that level of financial commitment. To this point, Craft-Bilt had only provided us general information regarding the Charlotte area market for sunroom additions and infomercial sales techniques.

- However, as luck or fate would have it, during our new hire interview process, we learned that our new sales person and one of our installers had actually worked for a Betterliving™ dealer who had operated in the Charlotte area. It appeared

Betterliving Patio & Sunrooms of the Central Carolinas in 2005

that the dealership had closed only a few years prior. This was news to us. During numerous meeting and discussions with Craft-Bilt, we were not provided any meaningful information regarding a prior dealer in the territory.

• Then, we experienced another revealing episode while touring potential facilities with the Craft-Bilt President prior to making a decision. The real estate broker was showing us a building located in a business park in North Charlotte. After getting a description of the type of business we would be operating, the broker indicated he wanted to show us another building. He rushed us over to another location in the same office park. He excitedly showed us a space which had an office area, a showroom and a 5,000 sq. ft. warehouse area. The building had not been leased since the previous tenant vacated the property. The broker recalled that the previous tenant stored extruded aluminum beams in the warehouse area. Earl and I looked at each other and then at the Craft-Bilt President.

• Following the tour and while enjoying some Carolina pulled-pork for lunch, Craft-Bilt confirmed that the building we had just seen was the location of the prior Betterliving™ dealer. The previous dealer was also based in the Charlotte area and had the same territory we had just agreed to service with Betterliving™ products. This discovery was quite revealing.

Certainly, we would now request all of the historical performance data available regarding the previous dealership and factor this insight into our business plan and overall operations strategy. But, learning of the prior dealer and this location in this manner moved us to a cautious and

Betterliving™ Patio and Sunrooms of
Central Carolinas' first Project

more observant state-of-mind regarding all aspects of *Project Better-Future*. We were sure that it was a location that the Craft-Bilt President and business development director had visited a number of times in the past, yet they failed to mention it to us in previous discussions.

- In August 2005, we proudly opened the Betterliving™ Patio and Sunrooms of Central Carolinas located at 714 Montana Avenue. The 2,000 sq. ft. building was located in a small office park.

We were able to lease this corner unit from a neighbor who was also a prior landlord. The building was located just off of I-85 and Beatties Ford Road in Charlotte, NC. It had easy access to both I-85 and to I-77. It was large enough to contain a nice office area and a small warehouse. The

Charlotte displaying products

warehouse was organized such that we could maintain, at the minimum, sufficient material to support up to five room orders. Surprisingly, we could also store the company trucks in the warehouse at night.

- Between August and November 2005 we successfully sold and built new patio and sunrooms. The first room we completed was actually in the state of Virginia. We agreed to sub-build the room with the Betterliving™ dealer in the area to give our new carpenter/installers some early experience with the more complicated gable designed rooms. Our construction sites ranged from locations in older and more established Charlotte neighborhoods to new outlying sub-divisions. We built rooms to the north in the Raleigh, NC area and down toward the coast in the prestigious Pinehurst area.

- As we moved into the winter, business began to slow down. We expected the winter months to be slower and had budgeted to retain all of our employees. However, we did not expect the level of increase in the cost of advertising. We also were surprised by the changes that had occurred in the local telemarketing environment.

- The majority of the sales leads in this type of business format were generated from calls received from potential customers immediately after viewing our infomercials. The cost of these types of television broadcasts vary from city to city and are based on broadcast times. In the metropolitan Charlotte market, the cost per minute had increased significantly over the past decade.

- The number of leads received per broadcast could be historically tied to the number of customer home visits [where 95% of room sales are made and orders taken] and the number of rooms sold. This is why we had always viewed this business as being more of a "numbers game" or a sales/marketing challenge versus a construction business.

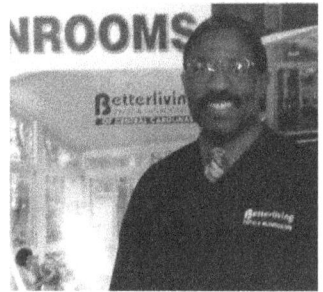

Earl in showroom

- As we approached the spring of 2006, we were spending more and more of our budget to purchase infomercials and receiving fewer and fewer sales leads per broadcast. I recall going into the office on a Sunday morning after an $800 Saturday night infomercial broadcast and finding only two phone requests for more information. That equaled $400 per lead. Ouch.

- In addition to the increase in "cost per sales lead" we noticed an equally troublesome and unexpected telemarketing reality. With the advent of caller ID, a higher percentage of calls returned to the potential customers by our sales staff [to schedule customer home visits] were going unanswered. Typically, we would attempt to return a call responding to an inquiry as many as 10-15 times in an attempt to make contact.

This follow-up activity, in itself, was becoming a more costly, but necessary, business function. We began discussions with Craft-Bilt in March 2006 regarding the need for assistance in deciphering the current Charlotte, NC sales and media market. To our dismay, we were not provided the type of support we were expecting. We had expected some fresh ideas such as hosting a local focus group to gain a better understanding of the current market. We also thought that it would be appropriate to revise some of the infomercials in an attempt to attract a broader set of potential consumers.

- With Craft-Bilt continuing only to recommend that we "invest more money in the same infomercials" and the fact that new print advertising was not working, we found ourselves with another potential *conundrum*. Except at this point in time, we had a couple of hundred thousand reasons to solve this riddle. The inevitable outcome would not only impact our life, but also the lives of employees and customers with whom we had taken deposits for pending orders.

- After a difficult strategy meeting in mid-April 2006, Earl and I met with our staff and shared our plan. We would make a significant investment in both television and print advertising. We would also increase the sales support effort between April and June. If we were able to obtain the business results we needed, we would target the items that worked and lay out broader plans to achieve the remainder of the year's goals. If we did not see improvement in results, we would be forced to *pull the plug* on current business operations and make a decision regarding future business options.

Outcomes

As we approached mid-May, it was becoming more and more obvious that the Carolinas market was, again, not a good one for a Betterliving™ Patio and Sunrooms dealership. Even with a significant increase in both television and print advertising, we were not able to realize the increase in orders we needed to justify additional investment. Earl shared with me an old adage that his father had shared with him when he was a young boy --- *"When you find yourself in a hole that's getting deeper and deeper with no apparent way out, then stop digging"*

Thus, in May of 2006 we began to take the necessary and prudent actions to shut down the operations of Betterliving™ Patio and Sunrooms of Central Carolinas. We were committed to completing all of the sunroom installations we had in backlog. We made sure that all of our customers were satisfied with their purchases. We also provided all of our employees with a severance package. The package included all outstanding vacation pay, two-weeks of salary and a COBRA option to maintain their healthcare policy. We paid off or worked out agreements with all of our venders. Having selected a month-to-month facility lease, we were able to navigate a rather soft landing.

Earl's niece, Glory and Sales Staff supporting a Home and Garden Show marketing exhibit

Without question, *Project Better-Future* turned out to be a project unfulfilled. However, it was not an experience without important lessons learned.

Even though our objective of establishing an enterprise which would be available for our family to leverage in support of their livelihoods had not been realized, the wherewithal, courage and passion required to take a *shot at a dream* was demonstrated.

During *Project Better-Future*, several family members were involved in the business operations. We also had the support and involvement of some dear friends. I am reminded of the words of an unknown author who pinned, *"Dreams are like stars, you may never touch them, but if you follow them they will lead you to your destiny."*

While Earl and I were wrapping up the closure of the patio and sunroom business and contemplating what might be next in our life, we were somewhat surprised when opportunities for both of us to return to Arizona surfaced. Returning to Arizona at that time would also put us in the position to get to know our young grandchildren. Our daughter had her hands full with a 5 year old and 10 month old. Within a matter of months, we found ourselves on another one of our life journeys as we returned to the Sonoran desert.

Thoughts Regarding Our Exploration

We had responded [and not simply reacted] to another major circumstance in our life. By implementing *Project Better-Future,* we had followed through on our objective to shape the best outcome to an undeniable circumstance. On one hand, we experienced a negative --- we lost money. Yet, on the other hand by recognizing when to "cut our losses" we may have significantly minimized a broader negative impact.

Nevertheless, by knowing that life is a continuum and not a collection of random events, we were *not surprised* that the years we spent together subsequent to *Project Better-Future* were more loving and the relationships we developed with our grandsons turned out to be *priceless.*

Maybe without our knowledge, we were not just building sunrooms but also following the stars which would eventually lead to *our destiny.*

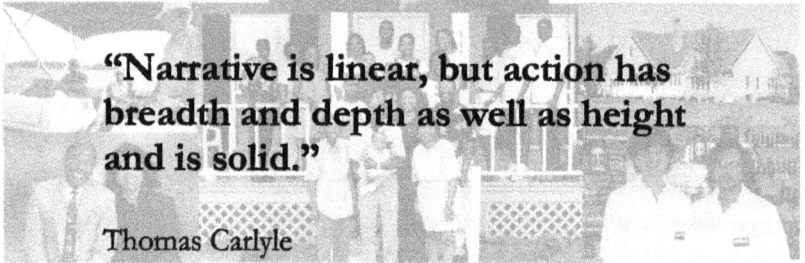

"Narrative is linear, but action has breadth and depth as well as height and is solid."

Thomas Carlyle

The Life Enrichment Model Application Guide

IMPORTANT: READ THIS BEFORE STARTING YOUR FIRST PROJECT

Use this Guide to apply the *Life Enrichment Model*™ to major events and the resulting circumstances that you may encounter in your life. Just follow the directions as set forth within each section. You should begin your project with Section 1.0, *The Framing Stage*.

You should not attempt to complete this project in one sitting. You should give yourself time to thoughtfully complete each section. It would be helpful to involve others, i.e. family members, friends, a professional coach or someone you trust, to be a part of what should be a confidential evaluation, analysis and course of action. Honest feedback from others can be extremely helpful in order to gain a more complete and healthier perspective of your circumstance. A complete or comprehensive view of all aspects of your situation is essential to confirming the facts surrounding the event.

You should give your project a name, i.e. *Project Make It Happen*. This will help to remind you that it also needs your attention as you go about other important daily tasks.

Your goal is to clearly and thoroughly understand your situation, your options and the potential consequences of your action or inaction. You should think through all the circumstances and potential opportunities that may be available to shape a more positive outcome.

Remember to consider all of your personal, professional and spiritual gifts as well as other resources that can be brought to bear to this situation. You should properly address all of the circumstances you are facing as a result of the event. Be mindful of what it will take to seize the potential opportunities and whether or not you are up to the task at this time.

Be diligent about planning the tasks and activities required to generate the desired outcomes. You must follow through on what must be done. Give this project the focus and priority it deserves. By starting and completing this project, we are sure you will make better decisions, feel better about the outcomes and experience the addition of richness in your life.

If we can be of any assistance with personal one-on-one coaching [via email, teleconference or in person], do not hesitate to contact us. There may also be opportunities for you to attend a local presentation or a group workshop in your area. You can find information regarding future presentations and workshops at www.richerlifeassociates.com.

Application Guide

Project Name_____   Date Started_____

1.0 The Framing Stage

Goal:	To extract a view or *frame* of your mind-set in order to reveal how you can place yourself in the best position to identify and examine opportunities embedded within a circumstance.
Input:	Review of the five stages of the Life Enrichment Model™ and detail descriptions of each model component to become familiar with their role in the modeling process.
Output:	An approximation of your current *perspective*. It is believed that this *approximation* is consistent with the "probable mind-set" you will take into your evaluation of the event and circumstance at hand.
Model Components:	*Framing Process, Framing Elements* and the *"Framing Query"*.

Application Steps:

1. *Summarize your thoughts regarding your current view or perspective of the situation at hand.*
2. *Complete Framing Query (See "Framing Query" Reference Sheet).*
3. *Grade your Framing Query results to determine Enrichment Platform (See "Grading the Framing Query" Reference Sheet).*
4. *Examine the Archetypes associated with the Enrichment Platform as determined by the Framing Query results (See "Platform Archetypes" Reference Sheet.)*
5. *Evaluate the thoughts you recorded in step 1 now that you have reviewed the Platform Archetype and note how your perspective of the situation may have changed at this point.*
6. *Move to the next stage, Opportunity Identification.*

Summary of my view and perspective of the situation at hand.

_____
_____
_____
_____
_____

Changes in my perspective regarding the situation after the Framing Archetype review.

_____
_____
_____
_____
_____

NOTES

Application Guide

2.0 The Opportunity Identification Stage

Goal:	Evaluate each circumstance to identify embedded potential opportunities. Then analyze each potential opportunity to detail and document the desired outcomes.
Input:	A sufficient exposure to the characterizations and insights embodied within the *Platform Archetype* suggested by the Framing Query results. This will aid in ensuring that all characterizations represented by the Framing Elements all have a "top-of-mind" position.
Output:	A list of circumstances, embedded opportunities and desired outcomes associated with the situation you are facing along with the insight and awareness gained through the evaluation and analysis process.
Model Components:	Step-One of the TWO-STEP Opportunity Identification Methodology.

Application Steps:

1. *Develop a list of circumstances, embedded opportunities and desired outcomes.*
2. *List ALL circumstances you perceive as apparent. Be specific and detail each opportunity and each desired outcome. Each circumstance should be unique but may be related to other circumstances.*
3. *Move to the next stage, Examination and Prioritization.*

List of Circumstances	Potential Opportunities	Desired Outcomes
1.	1. 2 3.	1. 2 3.
2.	1. 2 3.	1. 2. 3.
4.	1. 2 3.	1. 2 3.
5.	1. 2 3.	1. 2 3.
6.	1. 2 3.	1. 2 3.

NOTES

Application Guide

3.0 The Examination and Prioritization Stage

Goal:	To take the list of circumstances surrounding the situation at hand and decide which opportunities have the highest probability to enrich your life and are consistent with your capability to realize them at this time.
Input:	The list of "potential opportunities" developed during the Opportunity Identification Stage.
Output:	A list of the most actionable opportunities.
Model Components:	TWO-STEP Opportunity Identification Methodology and *Opportunity Priority Query.*

Application Steps:

1. *For each opportunity on your list, respond to each question of the Opportunity Priority Query. (See "Opportunity Priority Query" Reference Sheet)*
2. *Based on your response, select the most actionable opportunities which may shape a more positive outcome to the situation at hand.*
3. *Move to the next stage, Modal Exploration.*

Opportunity	Opportunity Priority Query Question #1		Opportunity Priority Query Question #2		Opportunity Priority Query Question #3		Actionable Opportunity?
1.	YES	NO	YES	NO	YES	NO	YES ☐ NO ☐
2.	YES	NO	YES	NO	YES	NO	YES ☐ NO ☐
3.	YES	NO	YES	NO	YES	NO	YES ☐ NO ☐
4.	YES	NO	YES	NO	YES	NO	YES ☐ NO ☐
5.	YES	NO	YES	NO	YES	NO	YES ☐ NO ☐
6.	YES	NO	YES	NO	YES	NO	YES ☐ NO ☐
7.	YES	NO	YES	NO	YES	NO	YES ☐ NO ☐
8.	YES	NO	YES	NO	YES	NO	YES ☐ NO ☐

NOTES

Application Guide

4.0 The Modal Exploration Stage

Goal:	Examine the list of most "actionable opportunities" to decide to either respond to the circumstance by pursuing the opportunity or to respond to the circumstance with another approach.
Input:	List of actionable opportunities from the Examination and Prioritization Stage.
Output:	An action plan for seizing each opportunity to be pursued. NOTE: A decision not to pursue the opportunity concludes the exploration process.
Model Components:	Modal Exploration process.

Application Steps:

1. *Examine the list of actionable opportunities using the Modal Exploration Process (See "Modal Exploration Process" Reference Sheet)*
2. *During the "Selection" mode of the process decide to either pursue the opportunity or not.*
3. *In the "Engagement" mode develop an action plan which will generate the desired outcomes.*
4. *Move to the next stage, Action Execution.*

Actionable Opportunity	Exploration Mode	Objectives and Outcomes
1.	Discovery	
	Deliberation	
	Selection	
	Engagement	
2.	Discovery	
	Deliberation	
	Selection	
	Engagement	
3.	Discovery	
	Deliberation	
	Selection	
	Engagement	
4.	Discovery	
	Deliberation	
	Selection	
	Engagement	

NOTES

Application Guide

5.0 The Action Execution Stage

Goal:	The Action Execution Stage tracks the execution of the actions developed and planned as a part of the Engagement Mode within the Modal Exploration Process.
Input:	Action Plan from Engagement Mode within the Modal Exploration Process.
Output:	Successful execution of actions required to address each circumstance and obtain the desired outcomes.
Model Components:	Engagement Mode within the Modal Exploration Process.

Application Steps

1. *Closely track the execution of all actions.*
2. *Note any follow-up actions that may be required.*

Action Item	Action Plan	Date Action Complete	Follow-up Actions
1.	· What · Who · Where · When · Desired result · Actual result		
2.	· What · Who · Where · When · Desired result · Actual result		
3.	· What · Who · Where · When · Desired result · Actual result		
4.	· What · Who · Where · When · Desired result · Actual result		

THE LIFE ENRICHMENT CONTINUUM™

The *Life Enrichment Continuum*™ is a paradigm that provides a systematic approach to characterizing [in a practical manner] the various environmental and human behavioral factors that come into play when any of us encounter circumstances in life.

The *Life Enrichment Continuum*™ is summarized in terms of its four basic *Enrichment Principles* and corresponding *Enrichment Challenges*.

Each Enrichment Principle sets forth a thought provoking observation regarding the environment and the forces at play when you find yourself in the position in life where you must encounter a potentially life altering circumstance. Integrating the Enrichment Principles into your *theater of thought* during these times will assist in establishing the *state of mind* optimum to properly identifying embedded enrichment opportunities.

The corresponding Enrichment Challenges constitute the knowledge-based objective or target you should attempt to achieve as you shape your responses to the circumstances which surround each event. Collectively, the Principles and Challenges establish the framework required to move you into position to get the most out of life's gifts and circumstances.

THE LIFE ENRICHMENT CONTINUUM™
PRINCIPLES and CHALLENGES

ENRICHMENT PRINCIPLE No. 1 - As we travel along the *Continuum of Life*, from one stage to the next, we accumulate insights and experiences which alter how we perceive ourselves, how we perceive others and how we respond to opportunities for life enrichment.

> **Enrichment Challenge -** *To recognize life enrichment opportunities presented to us as we travel along the Continuum of Life and to leverage the experience, maturity and wisdom we have accumulated by shaping our behaviors, perceptions and responses in order to take advantage of these opportunities.*

ENRICHMENT PRINCIPLE No. 2 - Negative outcomes as a result of encountering a circumstance, at any time along the *Continuum of Life*, can and most often impede life enrichment. Positive outcomes have both near and long term impacts and, in most cases, significantly enhance the richness [quality, fullness and abundance] in our lives.

> **Enrichment Challenge -** *To leverage the refinement and growth of our humanistic gifts (qualities) as we travel along the Continuum of Life in order to facilitate as many positive outcomes and eliminate as many negative outcomes as possible.*

ENRICHMENT PRINCIPLE No. 3 – The measure of richness in our life is based on the societal norms of the day and is an omnipresent perception which significantly influences our behaviors and responses to life's challenges and circumstances.

> **Enrichment Challenge -** *To maintain an awareness and perspective of the norms that are in vogue within society and to establish our own individual measure and perception of richness in our life as we respond to life's challenges and circumstances.*

ENRICHMENT PRINCIPLE No. 4 – Positive outcomes which result from taking advantage of enrichment opportunities later in life may have the potential of significantly offsetting the impact of negative outcomes at earlier stages in our life.

> **Enrichment Challenge -** *To enrich our lives to the fullest, we must not only recognize enrichment opportunities embedded within life altering circumstances but we must also take the actions necessary to ensure that we fully realize [gain the full impact of] as many positive outcomes as possible.*

The Life Enrichment Continuum™
A PARADIGM FOR LIVING A RICHER LIFE
Graphical Representation

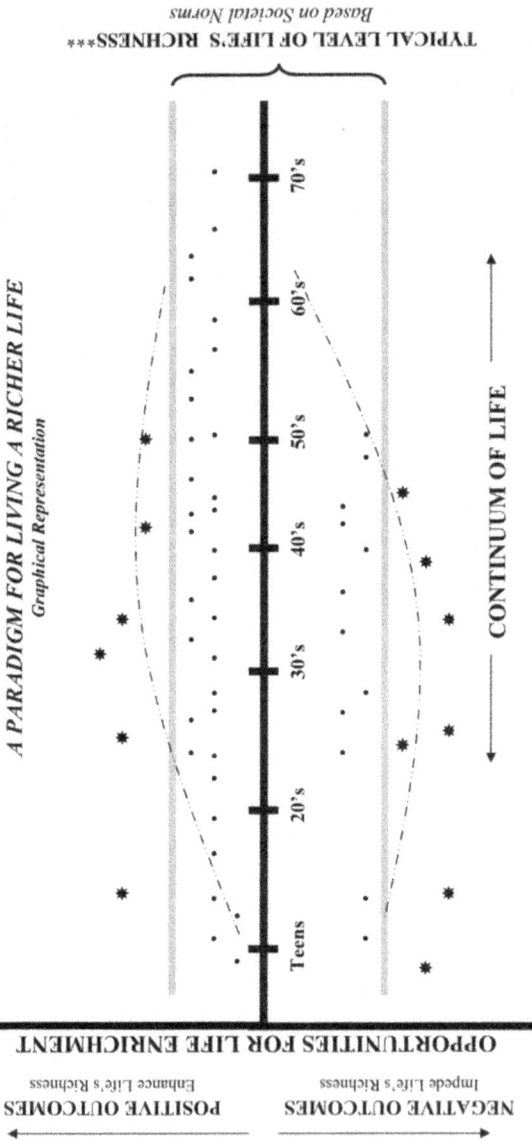

TYPICAL LEVEL OF LIFE'S RICHNESS***
Based on Societal Norms

Teens   20's   30's   40's   50's   60's~   70's

CONTINUUM OF LIFE

OPPORTUNITIES FOR LIFE ENRICHMENT

POSITIVE OUTCOMES
Enhance Life's Richness

NEGATIVE OUTCOMES
Impede Life's Richness

Legend

Opportunities for Life Enrichment along the Continuum of Life - embedded in circumstances as a result of major life events.

Outcomes to Circumstances which Change One's Life from Status Quo - either enhancing or impeding life's richness.

Perception of the Richness of One's Life - based on societal norms and shaped by individual actions or in-actions in response to inevitable circumstances in life.

***RICHER LIFE:\\'rich\'\'līf\ - a life full of good decisions, financial security, great relationships, loving family memories and a feeling of completeness.

102

Life Enrichment Model™

When properly applied, the *Life Enrichment Model*™ can become an exceptional tool to aid in identifying unforeseen opportunities and determining the paths available to you as you encounter potentially life changing circumstances. The results of the model's queries can help you get into *the position* [both mentally and practically] to make better decisions, take appropriate actions and to more consciously make the adjustments required to formulate your responses to shape more positive outcomes.

The model's construct utilizes figurative depictions and characterizations to provide valuable insights into the intangibles in your life at the time you encounter a major circumstance. The depictions and characterizations are generalizations and should be used *as a guide* to steer you in a most probable direction. However, when you merge these *generalities* with your own timely [internal and external] observations and sound reasoning, this combination gives you a significant advantage as compared to simple *reacting* and *going it alone*.

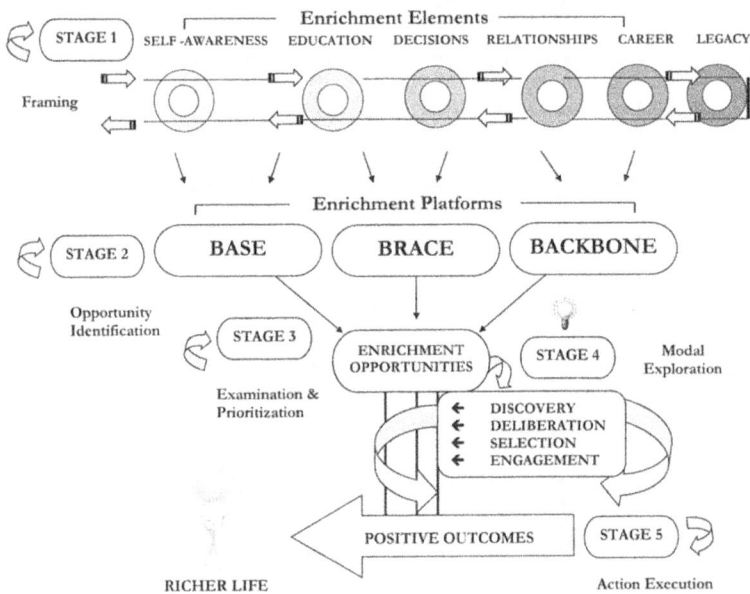

103

The Framing Process

The Framing Process systematically approximates your *mind-set* at the time you face major circumstances. The school of thought and general thesis of the *Framing* methodology is as follows:

"Your state of mind and perspective can be generally characterized by capturing an *inventory of your thoughts* surrounding six structural components, referred to as *Elements*. These *Elements* are believed to comprise an underlying system or structure that gives shape, strengthens and frames *who you are* and *what you are thinking* at the time you initially encounter a major circumstance in your life."

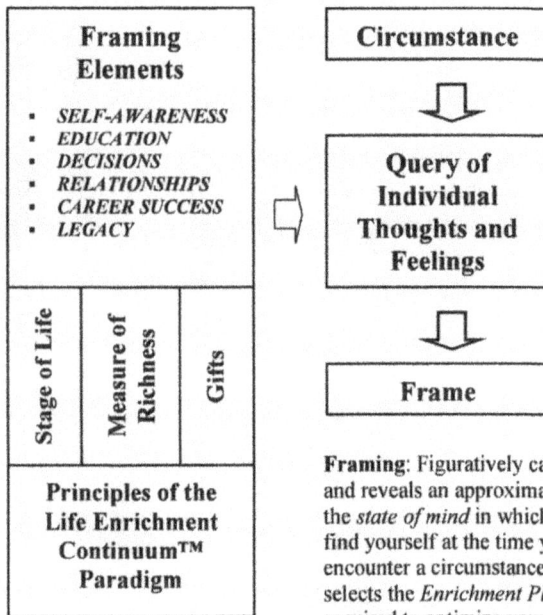

Framing Elements	Circumstance
• *SELF-AWARENESS* • *EDUCATION* • *DECISIONS* • *RELATIONSHIPS* • *CAREER SUCCESS* • *LEGACY*	⇩ **Query of Individual Thoughts and Feelings** ⇩
Stage of Life Measure of Richness Gifts	**Frame**
Principles of the Life Enrichment Continuum™ Paradigm	

Framing: Figuratively captures and reveals an approximation of the *state of mind* in which you find yourself at the time you encounter a circumstance and selects the *Enrichment Platform* required to optimize your *mind-set*.

104

The Framing Query

Provide "Best Answer" to each question below by responding with either True(T) or False(F)

Questions	Response (Circle one)	
1. Being self-aware allows me to recognize my emotions and their effects on my life.	True	False
2. Self-awareness limits my ability to accept candid feedback.	True	False
3. Even with a high level of self-awareness it is difficult to be confident about a situation when there are uncertainties and pressures involved.	True	False
4. Being self-aware means knowing more about others and how they view me.	True	False
5. A lower level of self-awareness makes it easier for others to understand me.	True	False
6. Having an accurate sense of who I am helps me decide what areas in my life I should improve.	True	False
7. Self-awareness helps to know my strengths but not cope with my weaknesses.	True	False
8. My emotional self-awareness makes me a more effective and intuitive decision maker.	True	False
9. Education is the knowledge of putting our potentials to maximum use.	True	False
10. It is not possible to be a life-long learner as you get older.	True	False
11. Learning is best done in the classroom.	True	False
12. There is more to good education than just demonstrating reading, writing, listening and speaking skills.	True	False
13. Even with an education, it still may not be possible to understand and remember new information.	True	False
14. I find it easy to adapt new methods to move forward.	True	False
15. I have obtained all of the education I need to be successful in life.	True	False
16. Life long learners are generally college educators with multiple degrees.	True	False
17. Generally, options are limited in most circumstances.	True	False
18. When options are limited I make decisions quickly since things most likely will not change.	True	False
19. I should always make a list of every possible outcome to all major circumstances I encounter.	True	False
20. I should never trust my intuition when making a difficult decision.	True	False
21. If I am not gifted in an area of competence that will help me make a better decision, I will make a good guess instead of bothering someone that I trust.	True	False
22. When it is difficult to choose between two options, I most often choose the one that is supported by both logic and intuition.	True	False
23. I should not focus on drawing insight and wisdom from every decision I make.	True	False
24. I do not have to feel comfortable with a decision if it is the correct one.	True	False
25. There are many qualities that make up positive and valuable relationships.	True	False

26.	Because most relationships are so complex, you have to accept what you get.	True	False
27.	I should always attempt to grow, leverage and maintain positive, valuable relationships.	True	False
28.	My interpersonal skills are important but not critical to a good relationship.	True	False
29.	I should concern myself with the impact of my decisions only if they involve family members and close friends.	True	False
30.	Knowing too much about others makes it difficult to grow a quality and positive relationship since there is little to learn and discover.	True	False
31.	A good relationship does not have any give-and-take when it comes to tackling challenging circumstances.	True	False
32.	I should take full responsibility for learning as much about the other person as possible.	True	False
33.	I am only partially responsible for my career because I will always need help from others.	True	False
34.	Having a successful career is not one of the most important factors in achieving my life goals.	True	False
35.	In order to keep my career on track, I must continuously update my skills and knowledge.	True	False
36.	Your current job or position is never the best place to start from when you are trying to move your career forward.	True	False
37.	If required, I have the power and determination to re-invent my career.	True	False
38.	A network of colleagues and acquaintances is good, but not a necessary part of managing my career and finding the best opportunities for advancement.	True	False
39.	You should always be prepared for the next opportunity.	True	False
40.	A successful career will be free of all negatives and disappointments.	True	False
41.	My overall success in life will define the future success of my legacy.	True	False
42.	There are only a few good reasons for valuing and leaving a legacy.	True	False
43.	Most people do not require some kind of assistance from others.	True	False
44.	To leave a legacy I simply need to give a gift to a charity.	True	False
45.	If I give to private foundations, I lose all personal control of who gets my help.	True	False
46.	Community foundations only accept large cash donations.	True	False
47.	A community foundation can pool funds and achieve economies of scale for investing, managing and granting philanthropic dollars.	True	False
48.	The act of giving itself reinforces who we are as human beings.	True	False

Grading the Framing Query and Selecting Archetypes

Step# [1] Place your responses in Column #2			Step# [2]	Step# [3]	Step# [4]	Step# [5]
Question #	Your Response (T or F)	Answer Key	Place a "X" next to the answers which match the Answer Key.	Total the number of "X's" for each of the three groups and place total in Box	Rank from 1 to 3 the "Totals" from Step #3 (With "1" being the highest total and "3" the lowest total).	Thoroughly review the Archetypes below associated with the LOWEST RANKED Group in Step # 4. This will optimize your *mind-set* prior to moving to the Opportunity Identification Stage.
1		T				
2		F				
3		F				
4		F			(If you have a" TIE ", review all Archetypes)	
5		F				
6		T				Platform: BASE
7		F				*Platform Archetypes*
8		T			( )	Awareness Anchor
9		T				and
10		F				Education Enthusiast
11		F		TOTAL	Group A RANK	
12		T				
13		F				
14		T				
15		F				
16		F				
17		F				
18		F				
19		T				
20		F				
21		T				Platform: BRACE
22		T				*Platform Archetypes*
23		T				Decisions Dynamo
24		F			( )	and
25		T				Relationship Rancher
26		F			Group B	
27		T		TOTAL	RANK	
28		F				
29		F				
30		F				
31		F				
32		T				
33		F				
34		F				
35		T				
36		F				
37		T				Platform: BASE
38		F				*Platform Archetypes*
39		T				Career Carver
40		F			( )	and
41		T				Legacy Leaver
42		F			Group B	
43		F		TOTAL	RANK	
44		F				
45		F				
46		F				
47		T				
48		T				

107

Opportunity Priority Query

1. *Do I have the physical, psychological & intellectual strength and stamina to take on what is required to move this situation, from where it is today, to where I envision it has to be, in order to obtain the value & richness I perceive it will add to my life, when fully realized?*

	YES
	NO

If No: Why Not? What are your concerns?

_____
_____
_____
_____
_____

2. *Do I have or can I acquire the level of resources [financial, moral & spiritual] required to seize the opportunity?*

	YES
	NO

If No: Why Not? What are your concerns?

_____
_____
_____
_____
_____

3. *If I decide to do nothing, am I ready to accept and live with the consequences that may arise as a result of this circumstance?*

	YES
	NO

If No: Why Not? What are your concerns?

_____
_____
_____
_____
_____

Two-Step Opportunity Identification Methodology

The TWO-STEP Opportunity Identification Methodology guides your thought process as you examine and prioritize opportunities and shape your responses to the circumstances. The methodology is designed to identify the most favorable starting point or optimal *platform* for entering into the opportunity examination process.

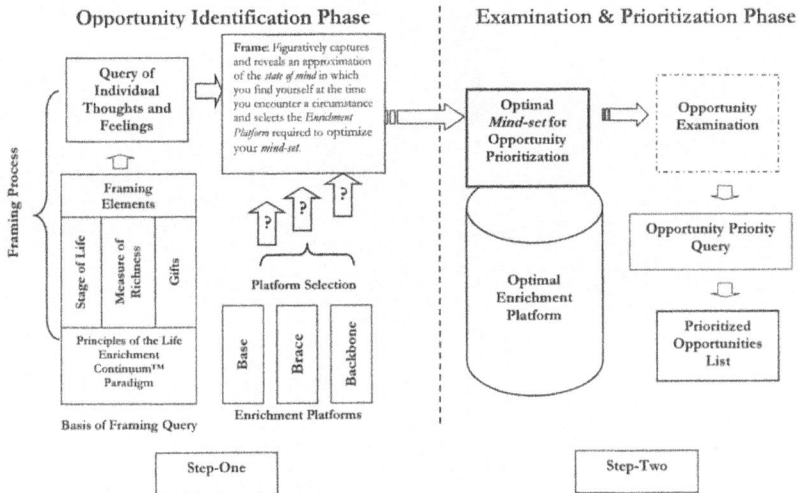

109

Modal Exploration

1.0 Discovery Mode

The circumstance(s) surrounding the event or situation are:

_____
_____
_____
_____
_____
_____
_____
_____
_____
_____
_____
_____
_____
_____
_____
_____
_____
_____
_____
_____
_____
_____
_____
_____
_____
_____
_____
_____

I can best describe the opportunity as follows:

_____
_____
_____
_____
_____
_____
_____
_____
_____
_____
_____
_____

2.0 Deliberation Mode

Summarize the tasks and activities that would be required to seize the opportunity and ensure the desired outcome.

I will need to do the following:

I need to get the following people involved for the reasons noted:

My concerns are as follows:

3.0 Selection Mode

Document the Pros and Cons associated with your ability to complete the tasks and activities required to seize the opportunity. After carefully weighing the Pros, Cons and your ability to execute what is required, then make a decision to either pursue the opportunity or to respond to the circumstance with another approach. A decision not to pursue the opportunity concludes the Modal Exploration process.

The Pros in this situation are as follows:

The Cons in this situation are as follows:

My Concerns with being able to do what is required to seize the opportunity are:

My Decision is:

Basis of my Decision is as follows:

4.0 Engagement and Action Execution Modes

Action	Responsibility	Date Started	Date Completed

Enrichment Platform: **BASE**
Enrichment Element: **SELF-AWARENESS**

ARCHETYPE
AWARENESS ANCHOR

I am the *Awareness Anchor*. I am emotionally aware. I clearly recognize my emotions and their effects. I know which emotions I feel and why. I recognize how my feelings affect my performance. I have a guiding awareness of my values and goals. I know my strengths and limits.

I am aware of my strengths and weaknesses. I am reflective. I learn from my experiences. I am open to candid feedback, new perspectives, continuous learning, and self-development. I am able to show a sense of humor and perspective about myself.

I am self-confident. I am sure about my self-worth and capabilities. I present myself with self-assurance. I have "presence". I can voice views that are unpopular and go out on a limb for what is right. I am decisive. I am able to make sound decisions despite uncertainties and pressures.

I know that an essential factor in maintaining genuine personal connections with others is through my self-awareness. Through my self-awareness I have the ability to perceive what is going on with me at all times. Since skill of understanding who we are is not taught in school, achieving my level of self-awareness is an extremely difficult assignment.

I became the Awareness Anchor and learned the skill of becoming self-aware through a high level of focus and observation. However, it was my strong desire to attract and cultivate authentic, meaningful and satisfying personal relationships in my life that sustained the effort required to truly know myself.

Over the years, I have learned that the more I understand myself, the easier it is for others to understand me. This has set the stage for more meaningful, rewarding relationships in my life.

Having an accurate sense of who I am helps me decide what areas of my life I can improve. I am able to produce high quality decisions by knowing my strengths and how to cope with my weaknesses. I am not hesitant to consult colleagues and subordinates that I trust to both gain a broader perspective and understand unique details.

My emotional self-awareness allows me to become a more effective and intuitive decision maker. I am able to read my "gut feelings" and use this to help guide timely decisions when facing difficult circumstances. I know who I am at this moment. I am the *Awareness Anchor.*

Enrichment Platform: **BASE**
Enrichment Element: **EDUCATION**

ARCHETYPE
EDUCATION ENTHUSIAST

I am the *Education Enthusiast*. I am aware of the demands of the global workplace. I know the needs of society are changing rapidly. I believe that education, being the knowledge of putting our potentials to maximum use, is key to a productive lifestyle in the 21st century.

I believe that education is more than collecting knowledge without understanding its value. I believe that the processing of knowledge fuels inspiration, visionary ambitions, creativity, motivation and my ability to bounce back from failure. I believe that we all gain true value of knowledge through life-long learning.

I am a life-long learner. I use my strong reading, writing, listening and speaking skills to achieve my life goals. I possess an awareness of what I need to learn and know. I leverage my education and desire to learn to succeed in life by managing day-to-day circumstances. I have worked hard to become interdependent and interpersonally competent. I believe in persistence and responsibility.

It is in my nature to be venturesome and creative. I set specific goals for myself. I understand the value of adopting powerful strategies for attaining my goals. I closely monitor my performance for signs of progress. I am sensitive to the need to sometime restructure my physical and social environment to make it compatible with my goals. I efficiently manage my time. I find it easy to adapt new methods to move forward and build valuable relationships.

I know that it is important to be skilled in identifying, retrieving, and organizing information. I am capable of understanding and remembering new information. I proactively demonstrate critical thinking skills and my ability to reflect on my own understanding. I am self-directed. I am self-regulated. I am self-motivated. I am reflective.

I understand the value associated with being curious and motivated. I recognize the significance of being methodical and disciplined. I realize the power of being logical and analytical. Yet, I know the importance of being self-aware and flexible. When I come face-to-face with difficult circumstances, I carefully assess the situation and ask --- What can I learn?

I am the *Education Enthusiast.*

Enrichment Platform: **BRACE**
Enrichment Element: **DECISIONS**

ARCHETYPE
DECISIONS DYNAMO

 I am the Decisions Dynamo. On my way to making good decisions I always list my options. It may appear that there is only one course of action, but I know that this is usually not true. Even if my situation seems limited, I always manage to identify alternatives.

I always weigh the possible outcomes to every major circumstance in my life. For every possible course of action, I list all possible outcomes. I then label them as either having a positive or negative impact on the richness of my life. One method I use to track this analysis is to place a plus sign (+) next to each positive outcome and a minus sign (-) next to each negative outcome.

I always consult my gift of intuition. If I am not gifted in an area which would help make a better decision, I will always seek input from someone I trust.

I must feel comfortable with all of the decisions I make. I will always make a decision and choose the best option available. I remind myself that making a final decision is always a difficult task. Thus, I focus first on the decisions on my list that are supported by both logic and intuition. My final choice always has more plus signs than negative signs and is always confirmed by my intuition.

I always monitor and evaluate the results and outcomes of my decisions. However, if I do not evaluate my decisions afterward, I will not learn anything from the experience. I need to know whether the outcome was what I expected. I need to know whether or not I would respond to the circumstance in the same way in the future.

In addition, I need to understand what I learned from each encounter with each circumstance.

As the Decisions Dynamo, I consistently focus on drawing insight and wisdom from every decision I make. My goal is always to ensure that every choice has a positive outcome.

Through my self-awareness, I know that regardless of my efforts, I may experience negative outcomes. However, I strive to always be aware of *what happened along the way.*

I am the *Decisions Dynamo.*

Enrichment Platform: **BRACE**
Enrichment Element: **RELATIONSHIPS**

ARCHETYPE
RELATIONSHIP RANCHER

I am the *Relationship Rancher*. There are many qualities that make up positive and valuable relationships. Good support, compromise and honest communication are just a few of the qualities I desire in all of my relationships. I believe in creating value in my life and contributing value to others.

My definition of value in a relationship includes the ability to grow, leverage and mutually benefit from the association. It also includes a balance between the ups and downs while expecting significantly more positives than negatives. I have learned that in order to grow, leverage and maintain positive, valuable relationships, I must first focus on developing my own relationship skills.

Strong relationship skills allow me to manage and always be in control of what I bring and what I take away from all my relationships. Over time, I have learned that what works best for me are strong communications, interpersonal, decision making and learning skills.

To sharpen my communications skills I speak so that others can understand me. That way, they do not have to guess what's important in my life and what I expect from a particular relationship. I listen actively so that I am sure I understand what's being shared and what's being asked of me. I strive for continuous improvement of my interpersonal skills.

I understand that I must cooperate with others and treat them in the same manner that I wish to be treated. I have found that I must work harder on improving my interpersonal skills as I advance in age and wisdom. It does not always pay to be the smartest person in the room. I am careful as well as cautious when it comes to decision-making. I take the time to clearly understand how my decisions will impact others. I am well aware of the need to give in order to receive. I am also mindful of the fact that all relationships are not equal. Sometimes the giving is to support one relationship and the value is returned by means of a different relationship.

I take full responsibility for learning as much about the other person as possible. The more I know about what each of us bring into a relationship the better I will be able to manage and control the unforeseen. I was taught early in life to really know someone, *make sure you are around for all four seasons*. I am very selective as to how I define and what I expect from my broad range of relationships. Each of my relationships has its three P's ---Place, Purpose and Position --- in my life.

In any relationship, there is going to be give-and-take as situations and circumstances change. Thus, I make sure that all my relationships are quality relationships. I make sure that they all are properly aligned with the richness I desire in my life. I am the *Relationship Ranger*.

Enrichment Platform: **BACKBONE**
Enrichment Element: **CAREER SUCCESS**

ARCHETYPE
CAREER CARVER

I am *Career Carver*. I know that in America today, more than ever, I am responsible for building my career and guiding it to the level of success that complements the richness I desire in my life.

I am a life-long learner. I know that one of the major factors for career success is to never stop learning. I know that my world is constantly changing and that just as in life, career success depends on identifying new ways of doing things. I know that in order to keep my career on track, I must continuously update my skills and knowledge.

I am a good listener. Because I am a good listener, I can learn things quickly and avoid many of the schools of hard knocks. I learn from other's experiences.

I know that my current job or position is the best place to start and move my career in the trajectory that I desire. I know that often very little separates the most successful people from the average person. I know that nothing comes free. I know that the best way to advance my career is to do my current job well and fulfill current responsibilities.

I am constantly building and adding to my network of colleagues and acquaintances. I know that my next career step might arise from my contact network. I spend quality time building new contacts and relationships. I never forget to maintain the relationships I already have.

I know that the best way to obtain valuable information from my network is to provide others with the information they are seeking. I am always prepared for the next opportunity. I maintain a current resume and update it regularly. I know that the next step on my career ladder to success may surface tomorrow.

But above all, when I find myself in a position where I am stalled in my career and my success is in jeopardy, I know that I have the power and determination to re-invent myself. I never lose sight of the fact that as we travel along the continuum of life, we will experience both negatives and positives in all phases of our life, including career success.

It is with this understanding that I know that true success in life is to increase positive outcomes and minimize negative outcomes. I know that, at times, success equals maintaining par for the course. I am *Career Carver.*

Enrichment Platform: **BACKBONE**
Enrichment Element: **LEGACY**

ARCHETYPE
LEGACY LEAVER

I am *Legacy Leaver.* I know that the key to success is to always start everything you do with an end in mind. I realize that this simple bit of common sense could really be applied to all aspects of life, including career, family, personal relationships and professional goals.

I believe that to live a life of passion and significance requires making noteworthy strives and achievements. As a legacy leaver, I express my personal values by integrating my charitable, family and financial goals.

I know that my overall success in life will define my legacy. I know that there are many reasons for valuing and leaving a legacy. Each is as important as the next. I see legacy giving as a responsibility owed to my community.

I know that most people require some kind of assistance, whether it's physical, financial or spiritual. I am well aware of local church congregation or food banks supplying meals during a tough time. I have seen how a scholarship has made a dream of college possible.

I have witnessed loved ones and friends receive compassionate care in local hospitals during illness or injury. As I travel along the continuum of life, I am reminded that more must be done to continue positive, humane acts of kindness and to sustain programs for personal enrichment.

I take advantage of a number of ways to be philanthropic. I feel good about living my life well and leaving a legacy.

I give to charitable organizations. My gifts to established charities provide direct support to those organizations such as schools, hospitals, arts and cultural institutions, human service agencies and religious organizations. My gifts to these nonprofit organizations vary in size. I give to private foundations. Private foundations allow me to retain personal control and flexibility over giving programs. My gifts to community foundations can be of any size, from as little as a dollar to thousands -- or millions -- of dollars. By pooling funds, community foundations achieve economies of scale for investing, managing and granting philanthropic dollars.

I know that when I give freely and without any expectations of a return, the act of giving itself reinforces who I am as a human being. I know that what I give unconditionally *will come back to me ten-fold* and will enrich my life. I am *Legacy Leaver.*

GLOSSARY OF TERMS

BACKBONE

BACKBONE is the third of the three Enrichment Platforms. It is the most substantial and sturdiest component within the Life Enrichment Model™. BACKBONE is anchored by the two *stabilizing* Enrichment Elements --- CAREER SUCCESS and LEGACY. They are characteristic of a mind-set cognizant of what it takes to achieve the level of financial achievement & self-actualization you desire in life.

BASE

BASE is the first of the three Enrichment Platforms. Base is the most fundamental component within the Life Enrichment Model ™. BASE is anchored by the two *foundational* Enrichment Elements --- SELF-AWARENESS and EDUCATION. These Elements, through Platform Archetypes, aid in focusing your thoughts on "Who am I" and "What can I learn" at the time you initially encounter a major life event. Having these thoughts *top-of-mind* should aid your efforts to capture a complete perspective of the situation, the surrounding circumstances and opportunities to shape a more positive outcome.

BRACE

BRACE is the second of the three Enrichment Platforms. BRACE is anchored by the two *action-oriented* elements --- DECISIONS and RELATIONSHIPS. They are characteristic of a mind-set cognizant of what it takes to strengthen the pursuit of your ultimate life goals and reinforcing prosperous alignments with others.

"CAREER SUCCESS"

CAREER SUCCESS is one of the two *stabilizing* Enrichment Elements which serve as anchors within the BACKBONE Enrichment Platform.

CONTINUUM OF LIFE

The Continuum of Life is the human life span viewed as a "continuous opportunity" for personal growth and enrichment. As you travel along the *continuum of life*, you acquire additional gifts, talents and wisdom as well as a deeper *awareness* and a broader *perspective* of yourself, your environment and others around you.

"DECISIONS"

DECISIONS is one of the two *action-oriented* Enrichment Elements which serve as anchors within the BRACE Enrichment Platform.

DELIBERATION MODE

The Deliberation Mode is the second mode of the Modal Exploration process. In the Deliberation Mode, you are enlightened by the development of a complete understanding of an enrichment opportunity which you have identified as a potential response to a circumstance at hand. This step of the process is completed by documenting *what will be required of you* and *others* in order to *seize* the opportunity.

DISCOVERY MODE

The Discovery Mode is the first mode of the Modal Exploration process. In the Discovery Mode the objective is to develop a concise summary and description of each circumstance surrounding the *event* or *situation* at hand. This activity is fueled by a thoughtful and thorough examination of all aspects of the situation.

"EDUCATION"

EDUCATION is one of the two *foundational* Enrichment Elements which serve as anchors within the BASE Enrichment Platform.

ENGAGEMENT MODE

The Engagement Mode is the fourth and final mode of the Modal Exploration process. In the Engagement Mode, you develop and execute the *action plan* required to seize the enrichment opportunity. While in this mode you will also perform the follow-up activity required to evaluate the actual outcome and its impact on your life's richness.

ENRICHMENT ELEMENTS

Enrichment Elements are core sub-structures that constitute the Enrichment Platform. As an aggregate, the Enrichment Elements influence what we think, how we think and how we perceive the circumstances we encounter.

ENRICHMENT PLATFORMS

Enrichment Platforms constitute the core foundation upon which the Life Enrichment Model™ is positioned. Within the model, the Enrichment Platforms figuratively represent the underlying social and economic structure inherent to the work ethic and dreams of the vast majority of the working populace. Each platform consists of two Enrichment Elements.

EXPLORATION MODES

The Explorations Modes are used to examine the enrichment opportunities which may be embedded within the circumstances that surface as a consequence of Life Events. The four Modes are characterized as the Discovery Mode, the Deliberation Mode, the Selection Mode and the Engagement Mode.

FRAMING

Framing is the act of capturing your state of mind at the time a circumstance is initially encountered.

GREATER GIFTS

Great Gifts are qualities which, as compared to other human gifts, more directly contribute to your ability to put yourself in a position to take the actions which will result in positive outcomes. The *greater gifts* are exemplified by the following traits: *Self-awareness*, *Imagination*, *Conscience* and *Independent Will*.

"LEGACY"

LEGACY is one of the two *stabilizing* Enrichment Elements which serve as anchors within the BACKBONE Enrichment Platform.

LIFE ENRICHMENT CONTINUUM™

The Life Enrichment Continuum™ is a paradigm that provides a systematic approach to characterizing the various *environmental*, *societal* and *human behavioral* factors that come into play when you encounter major circumstances in life.

LIFE ENRICHMENT MODEL™

The Life Enrichment Model™ embodies the concepts of the Life Enrichment Continuum™. The model is designed as a deductive and interactive tool to support your personal effort to enhance your ability to respond to events and circumstances in your life.

LIFE CIRCUMSTANCES

Life Circumstances can take on many forms and can surface either physically, mentally or emotionally. In general, they are conditions or facts that determine, or must be considered in determining, a *course of action* that must be taken to *respond* to Life Events.

LIFE EVENTS

Life Events are noteworthy happenings that can occur at any time throughout your life span. Most events in life are fairly common. Most result in minor changes in your life and in your lifestyle. However, there are events such as the death of a spouse, a long-term loss of employment, a permanent disability, a chronic illness, a home foreclosure, personal bankruptcy and a teenage pregnancy that can cause significant turmoil and change in your life.

LIFE'S GIFTS

Life's Gifts are the natural talents and qualities you are given at birth i.e. mental, physical, emotional, intellectual and sensual abilities as well as those that you acquire via education, experience and maturation as you travel along the *Continuum of Life*.

MODAL EXPLORATION

Modal Exploration is a systematic process which uses a series of custom designed methodologies, queries and approaches to identify, prioritize and examine circumstances in order to seize embedded opportunities for shaping more positive outcomes.

OUTCOMES

An outcome is what follows after you respond or simply react to a circumstance. *Positive* outcomes tend to significantly enhance the level of richness in your life and have both near-term and long-term impacts. *Negative* outcomes seem to always be accompanied with setbacks and have the potential of impeding your growth and prosperity.

PLATFORM ARCHETYPES

Within the Life Enrichment Model™, Platform Archetypes are standards used to illustrate the essence of qualities set forth by each of the six Enrichment Elements.

"RELATIONSHIPS"

RELATIONSHIPS is one of the two *action-oriented* Enrichment Elements which serve as anchors within the BRACE Enrichment Platform.

RICHER LIFE

A RICHER LIFE is a life full of good decisions, financial security, great relationships, loving family memories and a feeling of completeness.

SELECTION MODE

The Selection Mode is the third mode of the Modal Exploration process. In the Selection Mode you must make a decision to either *pursue the opportunity* or to *respond to the circumstance* with another approach. A decision NOT to pursue the opportunity concludes this exploration.

"SELF-AWARENESS"

SELF-AWARENESS is one of the two *foundational* Enrichment Elements which serve as anchors within the BASE Enrichment Platform.

THEATER OF THOUGHT

Your *Theater of Thought* at the time you face an unexpected Life Event consist of what you *think* and how you *rationalize* the circumstances that have surfaced as a result of the event's occurrence. Both, your thoughts and your ability to rationalize can be influenced by what is presently dominating your "top-of-mind" and can significantly contribute to how you initially perceive the situation.

TWO-STEP OPPORTUNITY IDENTIFICATION METHODOLOGY

The TWO-STEP Opportunity Identification Methodology guides your thought process as you examine and prioritize opportunities and shape your responses to circumstances. The methodology is designed to identify the most favorable starting point or optimal Platform for entering into the opportunity examination process.

VECTORED CONSEQUENCE

A Vectored Consequence is the result of applying your perspective to *frame* or *view* a circumstance for the first time. The origin of such a consequence [one with magnitude and direction] takes the form of a set of captivating questions which attempts to illuminate the *difficulty of the challenge* at hand [magnitude] as well as the *course of action* that should be taken [direction] in response to the circumstance.

"Most people can look back over the years and identify a time and place at which their lives changed significantly. Whether by accident or design, these are the moments when, because of a readiness within us and collaboration with events occurring around us, we are forced to seriously reappraise ourselves and the conditions under which we live and to make certain choices that will affect the rest of our lives."

Frederick F. Flack

About the Authors

Ervin (Earl) Cobb
Charlotte D. Grant-Cobb, PhD

The Cobbs are widely recognized as two of the nation's *rising-stars* among Self-Improvement, Relationships and Inspiration authors, lecturers and speakers.

The collective seriousness and wit of their work has been described as perfect for "those seeking personal growth, change and life enrichment but are not quite ready for Dr. Phil."

Their prior books include *Until I Change, Living a Richer Life: Getting the Most out of Life's Gifts and Circumstances, Pillow Talk Consciousness: Intimate Reflections on America's 100 Most Interesting Thoughts and Suspicions, Focused Leadership: What You Can Do Today to Become a More Effective Leader, Transition,* and *Navigating the Life Enrichment Model*™. Their newest video lecture series is titled, *Get Ready to Reap All the Richness Your Life Has to Offer.*

They currently reside in Phoenix, Arizona.

"There is no right or wrong way of living this wondrous journey, but if we can live it the best possible way we can, enjoying everything around us, being in "this moment", constantly growing and learning, appreciating and loving, we would be much richer for it."

Unknown

╫RICHER Press
An Imprint of Richer Life, LLC

RICHER Press is a full service, specialty Trade publisher whose sole goal is to *shape thoughts and change lives for the better*. All of the books, eBooks and digital media we publish, distribute and market embrace our commitment to help maximize opportunities for personal growth and professional achievement.

To learn more visit
www.richerlifeassociates.com.